Learn from the Bible, Book One

Add to Your Faith

Rock Mimms

CROSSBOOKS
PUBLISHING

CrossBooks™
A Division of LifeWay
1663 Liberty Drive
Bloomington, IN 47403
www.crossbooks.com
Phone: 1-866-879-0502

Scripture taken from the HOLY BIBLE, NEW INTERNATIONAL VERSION®. Copyright © 1973, 1978, 1984 Biblica. Used by permission of Zondervan. All rights reserved.

Scripture taken from the King James Version of the Holy Bible.

First published by CrossBooks 02/18/2011

ISBN: 978-1-6150-7756-4 (sc)
ISBN: 978-1-6150-7757-1 (dj)

Library of Congress Control Number: 2011923045

Printed in the United States of America

Contents

The old church sits on a hill
Empty.
Tired, worn steps,
Tear-stained pews,
The people no longer come,
But the Spirit lingers.

\- Rock Mimms

FOREWORD

While stationed in Washington D.C. as the Air National Guard History Program Manager, my wife and I taught a singles Bible study in our apartment. I had had the ideas presented in this handbook previous to this time, but it was at that time I began to actually put action to my ideas and used this topic as the source for the singles' Bible group.

For a long time since then I procrastinated on the idea of actually putting my ideas and studies into a handbook that could be of use to other people. I had a wake-up call on Wednesday, August 19, 2009, that reminded me that I should have already done this work that I felt God had put into my heart to do.

I went to a local fitness center for a short workout while my wife was having a pedicure a few blocks away. I walked on a treadmill for 16 minutes at a four-minute pace, which really was not a strenuous task for a person who really actually uses his gym membership regularly. After completing the short workout, I went to the computer and logged in the activity.

The next thing I knew was being aware that I was strapped onto a stretcher which was about to be loaded into an ambulance. I was later told that a couple of employees at the fitness center notice that I was unconscious and lying on the computer keyboard. They laid me out on the floor and said they could find no pulse, I wasn't breathing, and I was turning blue in the face. They immediately sent someone to get the defibrillators. Before the person returned, I apparently took a deep breath and began breathing on my own. They tried to get contact information from me in order to contact my wife, but I apparently made no sense of what they were asking and still do not even remember anything else from inside the gym.

Apparently when I was about to be rolled into the ambulance, I must have opened my eyes. One of the ambulance personnel must have noticed, and he asked me if I knew where I was. I replied, "Well, it looks like I'm about to be in an ambulance." I'm not sure how he liked that response, but I was able to give him my wife's contact information.

I was taken to the emergency room in a new hospital where they immediately began running tests: ultra sounds, MRIs, MRAs, a cat scan, electrocardiogram, and eventually an angiogram. When the results of the first ultrasound came back, my doctor came in and told me that I had an aneurism on my aortic artery: I was not to move, try to sit up, put my legs over the side of the bed, or anything because this aneurism could easily break. My wife had gone for a sandwich, so she did not hear this information.

The doctor immediately ordered an ambulance to transport me to the downtown Santa Rosa hospital for immediate surgery. About ten minutes later, with the ambulance personnel standing at the door, and again with me strapped onto an ambulance stretcher, the doctor came back to my bedside to inform me that my first MRI results were back and that the ultrasound results had shown a false positive reading on the aneurism and that I did not even have one. He cancelled the ambulance, and booked me into a room upstairs in the same hospital.

On Thursday morning the doctor informed me that he would be sending me down to the Santa Rosa Hospital again to have me undergo an angioplasty and have stents put into my heart. Once again he had me strapped into an ambulance stretcher and taken downstairs where the ambulance personnel were already waiting. Just before I was to be rolled into the ambulance, the doctor returned to inform all of us, including my wife and daughter who were waiting in our car to follow the ambulance downtown that he was again postponing my trip because he wanted to confer with my vascular surgeon. So again I was transported back upstairs to my former room to spend the weekend.

On Friday morning, my cardiologist came in again to tell me that I would be moved to the downtown hospital that day for the angioplasty on Monday afternoon. Finally, true to my doctor's latest word, I went into surgery as scheduled and had three stents put into my heart. I guess reality set in when I was going over discharge procedures on Tuesday and my cardiologist held his thumb and index finger about a quarter of an inch apart and said, "I believe that you were this close to dying."

I recount all of these to simply say that I believe that God gave me a wake-up call to do something that I believe He would have me do that I had been long procrastinating on, the actual putting into print the contents of this handbook.

Introduction

This study is based upon the concepts presented in the introduction of II Peter, "Grace and peace be multiplied unto you through the knowledge of God, and of Jesus our Lord, according as His divine power hath given unto us all things that pertain unto life and godliness, through the knowledge of Him that hath called us to glory and virtue: whereby are given unto us exceeding great and precious promises: that by these ye might be partakers of the divine nature, having escaped the corruption that is in the world through lust. And besides this, giving all diligence,

add to your faith virtue;
and to virtue knowledge;
and to knowledge temperance;
and to temperance patience;
and to patience godliness;
and to godliness brotherly kindness;
and to brotherly kindness charity (love)." (II Peter 1:2-7) (KJV)

The concept of adding indicates that one must already be in possession of something in order to add to it. The Bible tells us, "Without faith it is impossible to please God." (Hebrews 11:6) Therefore, we have to know that faith has to be the first step in a Christian's life. Next we have virtue, concerning which we are told, "All of us have become like one who is unclean, and all our righteous acts are like filthy rags...." (Isaiah 64:6) The only way to get virtue then is to receive it from God Himself.

The Bible clearly compares the natural birth of a new-born baby to the spiritual birth of a new-born Christian. Just as a baby can only take milk as nourishment for growth, a new Christian is only able to be nourished with spiritual "milk." Yet the baby normally has all of its parts for natural, healthy growth: a head, body, arms, legs, fingers, toes, and internal organs. Likewise, a new Christian has small amounts of the above spiritual attributes, but they are in small quantity and need to be developed as a Christian progresses though spiritual life. The Bible says, "When I was a child, I reasoned like a child. When I became a man, I put childish ways behind me. Now we see but a poor reflection as in a mirror; then we shall see face to face. Now I know in part; then I shall know fully, even as I am fully known." (I Corinthians 13:11-12)

As we continue to grow spiritually, we, in turn, add knowledge, temperance, patience, and godliness, all of which add to our own spiritual growth. When we add brotherly kindness and love, we are using our spiritual growth more and more for the benefit of others. We know that love is the highest of all because we are told, "And now these three remain, faith, hope and love. But the greatest of these is love." (I Corinthians 13:13). (NIV) A young Christian who has come to Christ in faith also comes in love, but that love is not usually such that the person is ready to lay down his life for his friends.

I do not believe that this list is just happenstance. I believe the whole Bible is the Word of God and is given with specific purposes, many of which we may never understand while here on earth. I picture this spiritual growth as a stairway up which God would have us climb while we are here on earth, ascending from faith at the bottom to love at the top, and, when we leave this earth, I believe that it will also lead us to heaven.

On the other hand, I can picture a stairway for the lost, including the lost world that begins with unbelief and grows progressively worse, passing through human desires, ignorance, lack of control, indulgence, impatience, evil, and eventually to both hatred and hell. (See illustration) This does not mean, however, that every lost person will wind up in a life of hatred, just as every Christian, while here on earth, will complete their physical lifetime at the top of the stairway in absolute love for one another.

Although most of the entries in this study only contain one or two scriptures to support the ideas presented, most of them really have many dozens of scriptures that support this idea of a Christian's spiritual growth. It is meant to be a starting point for further study and growth as a Christian. As a saved person continues to take on more and more aspects of a Christian life, I believe that each and every step continues to grow. For example, after a person accepts Jesus Christ through faith, that faith should continue to grow all the way through the final step of love. The Bible tells us, "Now we see but a poor reflection as in a mirror; then we shall see face to face.

Now I know in part; then I shall know fully, even as I am fully known." (I Corinthians 18:12) When we get to heaven, we will gain spiritually in ways that could never be gained while here on the earth.

This study primarily uses the New International Version (NIV) version of the Bible, but at times the King James Version (KJV) is used in order to incorporate more ideas by including the different terminology appearing in these two different versions.

Part I

The King's Highway

Spritual Growth Chart

Man's Byway   **The King's Highway**

Hell   Heaven

Hatred   Love

Evil   Brotherly Kindness

Ungodliness   Godliness

Impatience   Patience

Uncontrolled   Temperance

Ignorance   Knowledge

Human desires   Virtue

Unbelief   Faith

Faith

For further study: Romans chapter 3; Hebrews chapter 11; I John 5:1-12

Hebrews 11:1 defines faith for us by saying, "Now faith is being sure of what we hope for and certain of what we do not see." Faith is an absolute necessity to become a Christian. However, James reminds us that faith alone will not be sufficient when he tells us, "You see that a person is justified by that he does and not by faith alone." (James 2:24) I believe that God has a purpose for each saved Christian, and it is up to each one of us to find that purpose for which He has called us. Faith is only the initial step in salvation. "For we are God's workmanship, created in Christ Jesus to do good works, which God prepared in advance for us to do." (Ephesians 2:10) We are also told, "Without faith, it is impossible to please God." (Heb. 11:6)

Shortly after Christ's crucifixion, Christians began calling their members' organization "The Way." Jesus said of Himself, "I am the way and the truth and the life. No one comes to the Father except through me." (John 14:6) Just before Paul was saved on the road to Damascus, he searched out believers and threw them into prison. Upon one occasion he went to the high priest and "asked him for letters to the synagogues in Damascus, so that if he found any there who belonged to 'The Way,' whether men or women, he might take them as prisoners to Jerusalem. " (Acts 9:1-2) (See also Acts chapter 19, verses 9 and 23.)

Everyone must come to God through faith in Jesus Christ before he or she can begin the work He has for us. There are many aspects of faith which are spelled out in the Bible. There are also varying degrees of faith. At one point Christ acknowledged, "I have not found such great faith." (Luke 7:9) Elsewhere the Bible tells us, "He was amazed at their lack of faith." (Mark 6:6) How much faith is required? When His disciples asked why they were unable to drive out a demon from a young boy, Jesus told them, "Because you have so little faith. I tell you the truth, if you have faith as small as a mustard seed, you can say to this mountain, 'Move from here to there' and it will move. Nothing will be impossible for you."(Matt 17:20-21)

The following aspects of salvation take place when a person is saved, but not necessarily in the order presented.

Acceptance - "…whoever **accepts** me **accepts** the one who sent me." (John 13:20) "Here is a trustworthy saying that deserves full **acceptance**: Christ Jesus came into the world to save sinners—of whom I am the worst." (I Timothy 1:15) "Therefore, get rid of all moral filth and the evil that is so prevalent and humbly **accept** the word planted in, which can save you." (James 1:21)

Access - "Therefore, since we have been justified through faith, we have peace with God through our Lord Jesus Christ, through whom we have gained **access** by faith into this grace in which we now stand…." (Romans 5:2) "For through Him we both have **access** to the Father by one Spirit." (Ephesians 2:18)

Asking - "**Ask** and it will be given to you; seek and you will find; knock and the door will be opened to you. For every one who **asks** receives; he who seeks finds; and to him who knocks, the door will be opened." (Matthew 7:7-8) "…You do not have because you do not **ask** God. When you **ask**, you do not receive, because you **ask** with the wrong motives, that you may spend what you get on your pleasures." (James 4:2-3)

Assurance - "Those who have served well gain an excellent standing and great **assurance** in their faith in Christ Jesus." (I Timothy 3:13) "…Let us draw near to God with a sincere heart in full **assurance** of faith…." (Hebrews 10:22)

Baptism - "He went into all the country around the Jordan, preaching a **baptism** of repentance for the forgiveness of sins." (Luke 3:3) "Peter replied, 'Repent and be **baptized**, every one of you, in the name of Jesus Christ for the forgiveness of you sins. And you will receive the gift of the Holy Spirit.' " (Acts 2:38)

Belief - "They replied, '**Believe** in the Lord Jesus, and you will be saved—you and your household.' " (Acts 16:31) "But we ought always to thank God for you, brothers loved by the Lord, because from the beginning God chose you to be saved through the sanctifying work of the Spirit and through **belief** in the truth." (II Thessalonians 2:13)

Born Again - "I tell you the truth, no one can enter the kingdom of God unless he is **born** of water and the Spirit. Flesh gives **birth** to flesh, but the Spirit gives **birth** to spirit. You should not be surprised at my saying, 'You must be **born again**.' " (John 3:5-7) "For you have been **born again**, not of perishable seed, but of imperishable through the living and enduring word of God." (I Peter 1:23)

Children of God - "Yet to all who received Him, to those who believed in His name, he gave the right to become **children of God**." (John 1:12) "How great is the love the Father has lavished on us, that we should be called **children of God**! And that is what we are! The reason the world does not know us is that it did not know Him." (I John 3:1)

Christian - "…The disciples were called **Christians** first at Antioch." (Acts 11:26) "However, if you suffer as a **Christian**, do not be ashamed, but praise God that you bear that name." (I Peter 4:16)

Christ's blood - "In Him we have redemption through **His blood**, the forgiveness of sins, in accordance with the riches of God's grace that He lavished on us with all wisdom and understanding." (Ephesians 1:7) "And so **Jesus** also suffered outside the city gate to make the people holy through His own **blood**." (Hebrews 13:12)

Cleansing - "…because on this day atonement will be made for you, to **cleanse** you. Then, before the Lord, you will be **clean** from all your sins." (Leviticus 16:30) "If we confess our sins, he is faithful and just and will forgive us our sins and **cleanse** us from all unrighteousness." (I John 1:9)

Condemnation - "Whoever believes in Him is not **condemned**, but whoever does not believe stands **condemned** already because he has not believed in the name of God's one and only Son." (John 3:18) "Therefore, there is now no **condemnation** for those who are in Christ Jesus, because through Christ Jesus the law of the Spirit of life set me free from the law of sin and death." (Romans 8:1-2)

Confession - "That if you **confess** with your mouth, 'Jesus is Lord,' and believe in your heart that God raised Him from the dead, you will be saved. For it is with your heart that you believe and are justified, and it is with your mouth that you **confess** and are saved." (Romans 10:9-10) "If we **confess** our sins, He is faithful and just and will forgive us our sins and purity us from all unrighteousness." (I John 1:9)

Confidence - "Let us then approach the throne of grace with **confidence**, so that we may receive mercy and find grace to help us in our time of need." (Hebrews 4:16) "This is the **confidence** we have in approaching God: that if we ask anything according to His will, he hears us. And if we know that He hears us—whatever we ask—we know that we have what we asked of Him." (I John 5:14-15)

Conquerors - "...in all these things we are more than **conquerors** through Him who loved us. For I am convinced that neither death nor life, neither angels nor demons, neither the present nor the future, nor any powers, neither height nor depth, nor anything else in all creation, will be able to separate us from the love of God that is in Christ Jesus our Lord." (Romans 8:37-39)

Conviction - "When He comes, He will **convict** the world of guilt in regard to sin and righteousness and judgment: in regard to sin, because men to not believe in me; in regard to righteousness, because I am going to the Father, where you can see me no longer, and in regard to judgment, because the prince of this world (Satan) now stands condemned." (John 16:8-11) "For we know, brothers loved by God, that He has chosen you, because our gospel came to you not simply with words, but also with power, with the Holy Spirit and with deep **conviction**...." (I Thessalonians 1:4-5)

Eternal Life - "For God so loved the world that He gave His one and only Son, that whoever believes in Him shall not perish but have **eternal life**. For God did not send His Son into the world to condemn the world, but to save the world through Him." (John 3:16-17) "And this is the testimony: God has given us **eternal life**, and this **life** is in His Son." (I John 5:11)

Faithfulness - "Woe to you, teachers of the law and Pharisees, you hypocrites! You give a tenth of your spices—mint, dill and cumin. But you have neglected the more important matters of the law—justice, mercy and **faithfulness**. You should have practiced the latter, without neglecting the former." (Matthew 23:23) "His master replied, 'Well done, good and **faithful** servant! You have been **faithful** with a few things; I will put you in charge of many things. Come and share your master's Happiness!'" (Matthew 25:21)

Fear - "But I will show you whom you should **fear**: **Fear** him who, after killing of the body, has power to throw you into hell. Yes, I tell you, **fear** him." (Luke 12:5) "Since you call on a Father who judges each man's work impartially, live your lives as strangers here in **reverent fear**." (I Peter 1:17)

Forgiveness - "… for you will go on before the Lord to prepare the way for Him, to give His people the knowledge of salvation through the **forgiveness** of their sins…." (Luke 1:76-77) "For if you **forgive** men their sin against you, your heavenly father will also **forgive** you." (Matthew 6:14)

Gift of God - "But the **gift** is not like the trespass. For it the many died by the trespass of the one man, how much more did **God**'s grace and the **gift** that came by the grace of the one man, Jesus Christ, overflow to the many! Again, the **gift of God** is not like the result of the one man's sin: The judgment followed one sin and brought condemnation, but the **gift** followed many trespasses and brought justification." (Romans 5:15-16) "For the wages of sin is death, but the **gift of God** is eternal life in Christ Jesus our Lord." (Romans 6:23) "For it is by grace you have been saved, through faith—and this not from yourselves, it is the **gift of God**—not by works, so that no one can boast." (Ephesians 2:8-9)

Glory - "…all have sinned and fall short of the **glory** of God." (Romans 3:23) "We were therefore buried with Him through baptism into death in order that, just as Christ was raised from the dead through the **glory** of the Father, we too may live a new life." (Romans 5:4) "But grow in the grace and knowledge of our Lord and Savior Jesus Christ. To Him be **glory** both now and forever! Amen." (II Peter 3:18)

Grace - "We believe that it is through the **grace** of our Lord Jesus that we are saved…." (Acts 15:11) "Through Him and for His name's sake, we received **grace** and apostleship to call people from among all the Gentiles." (Romans 1:5)

Great Faith - "When Jesus heard this He was astonished and said to those following Him 'I tell you the truth, I have not found anyone in Israel with such **great faith**." (Romans 8:10)

Healing - "Jesus turned and saw her. 'Take heart, daughter,' he said, 'your faith has **healed** you.' And the woman was **healed** from that moment." (Matt. 9:22) "(Lord) Stretch out your hand to **heal** and perform miraculous signs and wonders through the name of your holy servant Jesus." (Acts 4:30)

Hearing - "Consequently, faith comes from **hearing** the message, and the message is **heard** through the word of Christ." (Romans 10:17) "Therefore, anyone who **hears** these words of mine and puts them into practice is like a wise man who built his house upon a rock….But everyone who hears these words of mine and does not put them into practice is like a foolish man who built his house on sand." (Matthew 7:24-26)

Holiness - "…repent and be baptized, every one of you, in the name of Jesus Christ for the forgiveness of your sin. And you will receive the gift of the **Holy** Spirit."(Acts 2:38) "…join with me in suffering for the gospel by the power of God, who has saves us and called us to a **holy** life—not because of anything we have done, but because of His own purpose and grace." (II Peter 1:9)

Hope - "For in this **hope** we were saved. But **hope** that is seen is no **hope** at all. Who **hopes** for what he already has? But if we **hope** for what we do not yet have, we wait for it patiently." (Romans 8:24-25) "May the God of **hope** fill you with all joy and peace as you trust in Him, so that you may overflow with **hope** by the power of the Holy Spirit." (Romans 15:13)

Justification - "He was delivered over to death for our sins and was raised to life for our **justification**." (Romans 4:25) "Consequently, just as the result of one trespass was condemnation for all men, so also the result of one act of righteousness was **justification** that brings life for all men." (Romans 5:18)

Liberation - "…the creation itself will be **liberated** from its bondage to decay and brought into the glorious freedom of the children of God." (Romans 8:21)

Life - "Whoever finds his **life** will lose it, and whoever loses his **life** for my sake will find it." (Matthew 10:39) "I tell you the truth, he who believes has everlasting **life**." (John 6:47) "In Him was **life**, and that **life** was the light of men." (John 1:4) "Just as Moses lifted up the snake in the desert, so the Son of Man must be lifted up, that everyone who believes in Him many have eternal **life**." (John 3:14-15)

Light - "For God, who said, 'Let **light** shine out of darkness,' made His **light** shine in our hearts to give us the **light** of the knowledge of the glory of God in the face of Christ." (II Corinthians 4:6) "But you are a chosen people, a royal priesthood, a holy nation, a people belonging to God, that you may declare the praises of Him who called you of darkness into His wonderful **light**." (I Peter 2:9)

New Creature (New Life) - "We were therefore buried with Him through baptism into death in order that, just as Christ was raised from the dead through the glory of the Father, we too may **live** a new **life**." (Romans 6:4) "You were taught, with regard to your former way of **life**, to put off your old self, which is being corrupted by its deceitful desires; to be made **new** in the attitude of you minds; and to put on the **new self**, created to be like God in true righteousness and holiness." (Ephesians 4:22-23)

Obedience - "To **obey** is better than sacrifice." (I Samuel 15:22) "Through Him and for His name's sake, we received grace and apostleship to call people from among all the Gentiles to the **obedience** that comes from faith." (Rom. 1:5)

Peace - "Therefore, since we have been justified through faith, we have **peace** with God through our Lord Jesus Christ." (Romans 5:1) "Let the **peace** of Christ rule in your hearts, since as members of one body you were called to **peace**. And be thankful." (Colossians 3:15)

Prayer - "If you believe, you will receive whatever you ask for in **prayer**." (Matthew 21:22) "Pray continually." (I Thessalonians 5:17) "Therefore confess your sins to each other and **pray** for each other so that you may be healed. The **prayer** of a righteous man is powerful and effective." (James 5:16)

Redemption - Christ **redeemed** us from the curse of the law by becoming a curse for us...." (Galatians 3:13) "In Him we have **redemption** through

His blood, the forgiveness of sins, in accordance with the riches of God's grace…." (Ephesians 1:7)

Repentance - "…unless you **repent**, you, too, will all perish." (Luke 13:3) "The Lord is not slow in keeping His promise, as some understand slowness. His is patient with you, not wanting anyone to perish, but everyone to come to **repentance**." (II Peter 3:9)

Rewards - "For the Son of Man is going to come in His Father's glory with His angels, and then He will **reward** each person according to what he has done." (Matthew 16:27) "And without faith it is impossible to please God, because anyone who comes to Him must believe that He exists and that He **rewards** those who earnestly seek Him." (Hebrews 11:6)

Righteousness - "Blessed are those who hunger and thirst for **righteousness**, for they will be filled." (Matthew 5:6) "For in the gospel a **righteousness** from God is revealed, a **righteousness** that is by faith from first to last, just as it is written: 'The **righteous** shall live by faith.' " (Romans 1:17) "This **righteousness** from God comes through faith in Jesus Christ to all who believe. There is no difference." (Romans 3:22)

Salvation - "**Salvation** is found in no one else, for there is no other name under heaven given to men by which we must be **saved**." (Acts 4:12) "Godly sorrow brings repentance that leads to **salvation**…." (II Corinthians 7:10) "And you also were included in Christ when you heard the word of truth, the gospel of you **salvation**. Having believed, you were marked in Him with a seal, the promised Holy Spirit." (Ephesians 1:13)

Security - "We have this hope as an anchor for the soul, firm and **secure**. It enters the inner sanctuary behind the curtain, where Jesus, who went before us, has entered on our behalf." (Hebrews 6:19) "Therefore dear friends, since you already know this, be on your guard so that you may not be carried away by the error of lawless men and fall from your **secure** position." (II Peter 3:17)

Separation - "This is how it will be at the end of the age. The angels will come and **separate** the wicked from the righteous and throw them into the fiery furnace, where there will be weeping and gnashing of teeth." (Matthew 13:49-50) " 'Therefore come out from them and be **separate**,' says the Lord." (II Corinthians 6:17)

Shedding of Blood - "For God was pleased to have all His fullness dwell in Him, and through Him to reconcile to Himself all things, whether thing on earth or things in heaven, by making peace through His **blood**, **shed** on the cross." (Colossians 1:19-20) "In fact, the law requires that nearly everything be cleansed with **blood**, and without the **shedding of blood**, there is no forgiveness." (Hebrews 9:22)

Sheep - "Therefore Jesus said again, 'I tell you the truth, I am the gate for the **sheep**....I am the gate; whoever enters through me will be saved.' " (John 10:7) "For you were like **sheep** going astray, but now you have returned to the Shepherd and Overseer of your souls." (I Peter 2:25)

Sin - "For if you forgive men when they **sin** against you, your heavenly Father will also forgive you. But if you do not forgive men their **sins**, your Father will not forgive your **sins**." (Matthew 6:14-15) "For all have **sinned** and fall short of the glory of God, and are justified freely by His grace through the redemption that came by Christ Jesus." (Romans 3:23-24) "If we claim we have not **sinned**, we make Him out to be a liar and His word has no place in our lives." (I John 1:10)

Sorrow - "...I am happy, not because you were made **sorry**, but because your **sorrow** led you to repentance. For you became **sorrowful** as God intended....Godly **sorrow** brings repentance that leads to salvation and leaves no regret, but worldly **sorrow** brings death." (II Corinthians 7:9-10)

Spirituality - "So will it be with the resurrection of the dead. The body that is sown is perishable, it is raised imperishable; it is sown in dishonor, it is raised in glory; it is sown in weakness, it is raised in power; it is sown a natural body, it is raised a **spiritual** body. If there is a natural body, there is also a **spiritual** body." (I Corinthians 15:42-44)

Submission - "**Submit** yourselves, then, to God. Resist the devil, and he will flee from you." (James 3:7) "Everyone must **submit** himself to the governing authorities, for there is no authority except that which God has established. The authorities that exist have been established by God." (Romans 13:1)

Thankfulness - "...Sing and make music in your heart to the Lord, always **giving thanks** to God the Father for everything, in the name of our Lord Jesus Christ." (Ephesians 5:19-20) "So then, just as you received

Christ Jesus as Lord, continue to live in Him, rooted and built up in Him, strengthened in the faith as you were taught, and overflowing with **thankfulness.**" (Colossians 2:6-7)

The Way - "Jesus answered, 'I am **the way** and the truth and the life. No one comes to the Father except through me. If you really knew me, you would know my Father as well. From now on, you do know Him and have seen Him." (John 14:6-7) "He (Paul) went to the high priest and asked for letters to the synagogues in Damascus, so that if he found any there who belonged to **The Way,** whether men or women, he might take them as prisoners to Jerusalem." (Acts 9:1-2)

Thoughts - "For who among men knows the **thoughts** of a man except the man's spirit within him? In the same way no one knows the **thoughts** of God except the Spirit of God." (I Corinthians 2:11) "When I was a child, I talked like a child, I **thought** like a child, I reasoned like a child. When I became a man, I put childish ways behind me." (I Corinthians 13:11)

Transformation - "Do not conform any longer to the pattern of this world, but be **transformed** by the renewing of your mind. Then you will be able to test and approve what God's will is—His good, pleasing and perfect will." (Romans 12:1-3) "And we, who with unveiled faces all reflect the Lord's glory, are being transformed into His likeness with ever-increasing glory, which comes from the Lord, who is the Spirit." (II Corinthians 3:18)

Transgressions - "As for you, you were dead in your **transgressions** and sins, in which you used to live when you followed the ways of this world and of the ruler of the kingdom of the air, the spirit who is now as work in those who are disobedient. (Ephesians 2:1-2) "But because of His great love for us, God, who is rich in mercy, made us alive with Christ even when we were dead in **transgressions**—it is by grace you have been saved. (Ephesians 2:4-5)

Trespasses - "But the gift is not like the **trespass.** For if the many died by the **trespass** of the one man, how much more did God's grace and the gift that came by the grade of the one man, Jesus Christ, overflow to the many! Again, the gift of God is not like the result of the one man's sin: The judgment followed one sin and brought condemnation, but the gift followed many **trespasses** and brought justification." (Romans 5:15-16) "The law was added so that the **trespass** might increase. But where sin increased, grace increased all the more, so that, just as sin reigned in death, so also grace might reign through righteousness to bring eternal life through Jesus Christ our Lord." (Romans 5:20)

Trust - "As the scripture says, 'Anyone who **trusts** in Him will never be put to shame.' " (Romans 10:11) "**Trust** in the Lord with all your heart and lean not on your own understanding; in all your ways acknowledge him, and He will make your paths straight." (Proverbs 3:5-6) "Whoever can be **trusted** with very little can also be **trusted** with much, and whoever is dishonest with very little will also be dishonest with much." (Luke 16:10-11)

Victory - "But thanks be to God! He gives us the **victory** through our Lord Jesus Christ." (I Corinthians 15:57) "...for everyone born of God overcomes the world. This is the **victory** that has overcome the world, even our faith." (I John 5:4)

VIRTUE

For further study: Luke chapter 6

Once we have come to Christ for our salvation through faith, He expects a different kind of behavior from us. "Therefore, if anyone is in Christ, he is a new creation; the old has gone, the new has come!" (II Corinthians 5:17) Our faith should continue to increase as we continue to progress in our Christian lives. Our behavior is crucial if we expect to win others to a saving knowledge of Jesus Christ. If Christ has truly come into our hearts through faith, then our hearts will be changed by His spirit. Matthew tells us, "Blessed are the pure in heart, for they shall see God." (Matthew 5:8) and "...For out of the overflow of the heart the mouth speaks." (Matthew 12:34)

We do not have our own goodness, but only that goodness given to us by God Himself. Mark tells us, "...No one is good—except God alone." (Mark 10:18) So our goodness all comes from God. James tells us, "Every good and perfect gift is from above, coming down from the Father of the heavenly lights, who does not change like shifting shadows." (James 1:17)

This is not an all-inclusive list, but I believe God expects something of us after we have taken on the name Christian.

Abstinence - "...we should write to them, telling them to **abstain** from food polluted by idols, from sexual immorality, from the meat of strangled animals, and from blood." (Acts 15:20) "Dear friends, I urge you, as aliens and strangers in the world, to **abstain** from sinful desires which war against our soul. Live such good lives among the pagans that, though they accuse you of doing wrong, they may see your good deeds and glorify God on the day he visits us." (I Peter 2:11-12)

Approval - "For the kingdom of God is not a matter of eating and drinking, but of righteousness, peace, and joy in the Holy Spirit, because anyone who serves Christ in this way is pleasing to God and **approved** by men." (Romans 14:17-18) "Do your best to present yourself to God as one **approved**, a workman who does not need to be ashamed and who correctly handles the word of truth." (II Timothy 2:15)

Christian friends - "You are my **friends** if you do what I command. I no longer call you servants, because a servant does not know his master's business. Instead, I have called you **friends**, for everything that I learned from my Father I have made known to you." (John 15:14-15) "…don't you know that **friendship** with the world is hatred toward God? Anyone who chooses to be a **friend** of the world becomes an enemy of God." (James 4:4)

Cleanness (Cleanliness) - "First **clean** the inside of the cup and dish, and then the outside also will be **clean**." (Matthew 23:26) "Let us draw near to God with a sincere heart in full assurance of faith, having our hearts sprinkled to **cleanse** us from a guilty conscience and having our bodies washed with pure water." (Hebrews 10:22)

Conscience - "The goal of this command is love, which comes from a pure heart and a good **conscience** and a sincere faith." (I Timothy 1:5) "…this water symbolized baptism that now saves you also—not the removal of dirt from the body but the pledge of a good **conscience** toward God. It saves you by the resurrection of Jesus Christ…." (I Peter 3:21)

Desires (Cravings) - "Those who live according to the sinful nature have their minds set on what that nature **desires**; but those who live in accordance with Spirit have their minds set on what the Spirit **desires**." (Romans 8:5) "Like newborn babies, **crave** pure spiritual milk so that by it you may grow up in your salvation, now that you have tasted that the Lord is good." (I Peter 2:2-3)

Faithfulness - "Now it is required that those who have been given a trust must prove **faithful**." (I Corinthians 4:2) "But the fruit of the Spirit is love, joy, peace, patience, kindness, goodness, **faithfulness**, gentleness and self-control." (Galatians 5:22)

Forgiveness - "For if you **forgive** men when they sin against you, your heavenly Father will also **forgive** you. But if you do not **forgive** men their sins, you Father will not **forgive** you sins." (Matthew 6:14-15) "Peter replied, 'Repent and be baptized, every one of you, in the name of Jesus Christ for the **forgiveness** of your sins. And you will receive the gift of the Holy Spirit.' " (Acts 2:38)

Gentleness - "Let your **gentleness** be evident to all." (Philippians 4:5) "But in your hearts set apart Christ as Lord. Always be prepared to give an answer to everyone who asks you to give the reason for the hope that you have. But do this with **gentleness** and respect." (I Peter 3:15)

God's will - "Whosoever does **God's will** is my brother and sister and mother." (Mark 3:35) "And He who searches our hearts knows the mind of the Spirit, because the Spirit intercedes for the saints in accordance with **God's will**." (Romans 8:27)

Godliness (Holiness) - "…that we may live peaceful and quiet lives in all **godliness** and **holiness**." (I Timothy 2:2) "Beyond all question, the mystery of **godliness** is great: He appeared in a body, was vindicated by the Spirit, was seen by angels, was preached among the nations, was believed on in the world, was taken up in glory." (I Timothy 3:16)

Integrity - "The **integrity** of the upright guides them…." (Proverbs 11:3) "In everything set them an example by doing what is good. In your teaching show **integrity**, seriousness and soundness of speech that cannot be condemned, so that those who oppose you may be ashamed because they have nothing bad to say about us." (Titus 2:7-8)

Meditation - "Do not let the Book of the Law depart from your mouth; **meditate** on it day and night, so that you may be careful to do everything written in it. Then you will be prosperous and successful." (Joshua 1:8) "May the words of my mouth and the **meditation** of my heart be pleasing in your sight, O Lord, my Rock and my Redeemer." (Psalm 19:14)

Obedience - "…To **obey** is better than sacrifice, and to heed is better than the fat of rams." (I Samuel 15:22) "Don't you know that when you offer yourselves to someone to **obey** him as slaves, you are slaves to the one whom you **obey**—whether you are slaves to sin, which leads to death, or to **obedience**, which leads to righteousness?" (Romans 6:16) "…We take captive every thought to make it **obedient** to Christ…." (II Corinthians 10:5)

Purification - "Since we have these promises, dear friends, let us **purify** ourselves from everything that contaminates body and spirit, perfecting holiness out of reverence for God. (II Corinthians 7:1) "If we confess our sins, He is faithful and just and will forgive us our sins and **purity** us from all unrighteousness." (I John 1:9)

Rejoicing - "…**rejoice** that your names are written in heaven." (Luke 10:20)"…we **rejoice** in the hope and of the glory of God. Not only so, but we also **rejoice** in our sufferings, because we know that suffering produces perseverance…." (Romans 5:2-3) "**Rejoice** in the Lord always. I will say it again: **Rejoice!**" (Philippians 4:4)

Testifying (Testimony) - "So do not be ashamed to **testify** about our Lord…." (II Timothy 1:8) "For there are three that **testify**: the Spirit, the water and the blood; and the three are in agreement. We accept man's **testimony**, but God's **testimony** is greater because it is the **testimony** of God, which He has given about His Son." (I John 5:7)

Thanksgiving - "And whatever you do, whether in word or deed, do it all in the name of the Lord Jesus, **giving thanks** to God the Father through Him." (Colossians 3:17) "I urge, then, first of all, that requests, prayers, intercession and **thanksgiving** be made for everyone." (I Timothy 2:1)

Tithing (Giving) - "As soon as the order went out, the Israelites generously **gave** the firstfruits of the grain, new wine, oil and honey and all that the fields produced. They brought a great amount, a **tithe** of everything." (II Chronicles 31:5-6) "Bring the whole **tithe** into the storehouse, that there may be food in my house…." (Malachi 3:10) "Each man should **give** what he has decided in his heart to **give**, not reluctantly or under compulsion, for God loves a cheerful **giver**." (II Corinthians 9:7)

Truth - "To the Jews who had believed Him, Jesus said, 'If you hold to my teaching, you are really my disciples. Then you will know the **truth**, and the **truth** will set you free.' " (John 8:31-32) "Dear children, let us not love with words or tongue but with actions and in **truth**." (I John 3:18)

Worship - "…For it is written: '**Worship** the Lord your God, and serve Him only." (Matthew 4:10) "Therefore, since we are receiving a kingdom that cannot be shaken, let us be thankful, and so **worship** God acceptably with reverence and awe, for our God is a consuming fire." (Hebrews 12:28-29)

"and to virtue"

KNOWLEDGE

For further study: I Corinthians chapter 8; I Peter chapter 1

In this study of knowledge, I will consider knowledge as learning and wisdom as the application of that learning. Paul tells the Colossians, "For this reason, since the day we heard about you, we have not stopped praying for you and asking God to fill you with the knowledge of His will through all spiritual wisdom and understanding." (Colossians 1:9) Likewise, we need to be filled with the knowledge of God the Father, Jesus the Son, and the Holy Spirit.

Knowledge is always the truth. Many may believe a lie to be the truth, but that does not make it the truth. Repeatedly in the gospels, Jesus teaches the disciples by saying, "I tell you the truth…." (thirty times in Matthew alone)(NIV) Therefore this study considers knowledge and truth to be one and the same. Jesus' first ministry to mankind was teaching in the temple while He was yet a young boy.

Certainty (Sureness) - "…It seemed good also to me to write an orderly account for you…so that you may know the **certainty** of the things you have been taught." (Luke 1:3-4) "Now faith is being **sure** of what we hope for and **certain** of what we do not see." (Hebrews 11:1)

Consideration - "Do nothing out of selfish ambition or vain conceit, but in humility **consider** others better than yourselves." (Philippians 2:3) "But the wisdom that comes from is first of all pure; then peace-loving, **considerate**, submissive, full of mercy and good fruit, impartial and sincere. Peacemakers who sow in peace raise a harvest of righteousness." (James 3:17)

Counsel (Advice) - "**Counsel** and sound judgment are mine; I have understanding and power." (Proverbs 8:14) "Listen to advice and accept instruction, and in the end you will be wise." (Proverbs 19:20)

Discretion - "For wisdom will enter your heart, and knowledge will be pleasant to your soul. **Discretion** will protect you, and understanding will guard you." (Proverbs 2:10-12) "I, wisdom, dwell together with prudence; I possess knowledge and **discretion**." (Proverbs 8:12)

Enlightenment - "For You will **light** my lamp; the Lord my God will **enlighten** my darkness." (Psalm 18:28) "I pray also that the eyes of your heart may be **enlightened** in order that you may know the hope to which He has called you, the riches of His glorious inheritance in the saints.... (Ephesians 1:18)

Fullness - "... (Be) **filled** with the fruit of righteousness that comes through Jesus Christ—to the glory and praise of God." (Philippians 1:11) "But the wisdom that comes from heaven is first of all pure; then peace-loving, considerate, submissive, **full** of mercy and good fruit, impartial and sincere." (James 3:17)

Humility - "Do nothing out of selfish ambition or vain conceit, but in **humility**, consider others better than yourselves." (Philippians 2:3) "Who is wise and understanding among you? Let him show it by his good life, by deeds done in the **humility** that comes from wisdom." (James 3:13)

Hunger - "Blessed are those who **hunger** and thirst for righteousness, for they will be filled." (Matthew 5:6) "Blessed are you who **hunger** now, for you shall be filled. Blessed are you who weep now, for you shall laugh." (Luke 6:21)

Insight (Discernment) - "And this is my prayer: that your love may abound more and more in knowledge and depth of **insight**, so that you may be able to **discern** what is best and may be pure and blameless until the day of Christ, filled with the fruit of righteousness that comes through Jesus Christ—to the glory and praise of God." (Philippians 1:9-10) "Reflect on what I am saying, for the Lord will give you **insight** into all this." (II Timothy 2:7)

Instruction - "Choose my **instruction** instead of silver, knowledge rather than choice gold...." (Proverbs 8:10) "For God did not call us to be impure, but to live a holy life. Therefore, he who rejects this **instruction** does not reject man but God, who gives you His Holy Spirit." (I Thessalonians 4:7-8)

Learning - "Take my yoke upon you and **learn** from me, for I am gentle and humble in heart, and you will find rest for your souls." (Matthew 11:29) "But as for you, continue in what you have **learned** and have become convince of, because you know those from whom you **learned** it, and how from infancy you have known the Holy Scriptures, which are able to make you wise for salvation through faith in Christ Jesus." (II Timothy 3:14-15)

Listening - "It is written in the prophets: 'They will all be taught by God.' Everyone who **listens** to the Father and learns from Him comes to me." (John 6:45) "We know that God does not **listen** to sinners. He **listens** to the godly man who does His will." (John 9:31) "My sheep **listen** to my voice; I know them, and they follow me." (John 10:27)

Maturity - "We do, however, speak a message of wisdom among the **mature**, but not the wisdom of this age or of the rulers of this age, who are coming to nothing. No, we speak of God's secret wisdom, a wisdom that has been hidden and that God destined for our glory before time began." (I Corinthians 2:6-7) "...to prepare God's people for works of service, so that the body of Christ may be built up until we all reach unity in the faith and in the knowledge of the Son of God and become **mature**, attaining to the whole measure of the fullness of Christ." (Ephesians 4:12-13)

Remembering (Remembrance) - "Do you have eyes but fail to see, and ears but fail to hear? And don't you **remember**?" (Mark 8:18) "And He took the bread, gave thanks and broke it, and gave it to them, saying, 'This is my body, given for you; do this in **remembrance** of me.' " (Luke 22:19) "**Remember**, therefore, what you have received and heard; obey it, and repent." (Revelation 3:3)

Revelations - "For in the gospel a righteousness from God is **revealed**, a righteousness that is by faith from first to last, just as it is written: 'The righteous will live by faith.' " (Romans 1:17) "Surely you have heard about the administration of God's grace that was given to me for you, that is, the mystery made known by **revelation**, as I have already written briefly. In reading this, then, you will be able to understand my insight into the mystery of Christ, which was not made known to men in other generations as it has been **revealed** by the Spirit of God's holy apostles and prophets." (Ephesians 3:2-5)

Scripture - "Until I come, devote yourself to the public reading of **Scripture**, to preaching and to teaching." (I Timothy 4:13) "All **Scripture** is God-breathed and is useful for teaching, rebuking, correcting and training in righteousness, so that the man of God may be thoroughly equipped for every good work." (II Timothy 3:16-17)

Spirit of Truth - "And I will ask the Father, and He will give you another Counselor to be with you forever—the **Spirit of Truth**. The world cannot accept Him because it neither see Him nor knows Him. But you know him, for He lives with you and will be in you." (John 14:16-17) "But when He, the **Spirit of Truth**, comes, He will guide you into all **truth**. He will not speak on His own; He will speak only what He hears, and He will tell you what is yet to come. He will bring glory to me by taking from what is mine and making it known to you." (John 16:13-14) "We are from God, and whoever knows God listens to us; but whoever is not from God does not listen to us. This is how we recognize the **Spirit of Truth** and the spirit of falsehood." (I John 4:6)

Spiritual food (Solid food) - "They all ate the same **spiritual food** and drank the same spiritual drink; for they drank from the **spiritual** rock that accompanied then, and that rock was Christ." (I Corinthians 9:3-4) "Anyone who lives on milk, being still an infant, is not acquainted with the teaching about righteousness, but **solid food** is for the mature, who by constant use have trained themselves to distinguish good from evil." (Hebrews 5:13-14)

Stillness - "Be **still** before the Lord and wait patiently for Him; do not fret when men succeed in their ways, when they carry out their wicked schemes." (Psalm 37:7) "Be **still** and know that I am God...." (Psalm 46:10)

Strength - "He answered, 'Love the Lord your God with all your heart and with all your soul and with all your **strength** and with all your mind,' and, 'Love your neighbor as yourself.' " (Luke 10:27)"If anyone speaks, he should do it as one speaking the very words of God If anyone serves, he should do it with the **strength** God provides...." (I Peter 4:11)

Study - "You diligently **study** the scriptures because you think that by them you possess eternal life. These are the scriptures that testify about Me, yet you refuse to come to Me to have life." (John 5:39) "**Study** to show yourself approved unto God, a workman that needs not to be ashamed, rightly dividing the word of truth." (II Timothy 2:15)

Submission - "Submit to one another out of reverence for Christ." (Ephesians 5:21) "Submit yourselves, then, to God. Resist the devil, and he will flee from you." (James 4:7)

Teachers - "And in the church God has appointed first of all apostles, second prophets, third **teachers**, then workers of miracles, also those having gifts of healing, those able to help others, those with gifts of administration, and those speaking in different kinds of tongues." (I Corinthians 12:28) "Not many of you should presume to be **teachers**, my brothers, because you know that we who **teach** will be judged more strictly." (James 3:1)

Teaching - "Anyone who breaks one of the least of these commandments and **teaches** others to do the same will be called least in the kingdom of heaven, but whoever practices and **teaches** these commands will be called great in the kingdom of heaven." (Matthew 5:19) "Therefore go and make disciples of all nations, baptizing them in the name of the Father and of the Son and of the Holy Spirit, and **teaching** them to obey everything I have commanded you. And surely I am with you always, to the very end of the age." (Matthew 28:19-20)

Thirst - "Blessed are those who hunger and **thirst** after righteousness, for they shall be filled." (Matthew 5:6) "Then Jesus declared, 'I am the bread of life. He who comes to me will never go hungry, and he who believes in me will never be **thirsty**.' " (John 6:35)

Truth - "For we cannot do anything against the **truth**, but only for the **truth**." (II Corinthians 13:8) "God our Savior…wants all men to be saved and come to a knowledge of the **truth**." (I Timothy 2:3-4)

Understanding - "…we have not stopped praying for you and asking God to fill you with the knowledge of His will through all spiritual wisdom and **understanding**." (Colossians 1:9) "Who is wise and **understanding** among you? Let him show it by his good life, by deeds done in the humility that comes from wisdom." (James 3:13)

Wisdom - "…**wisdom** is more precious than rubies. I, **wisdom**, dwell together with prudence; I possess knowledge and discretion." (Proverbs 8:11-12) "We do, however, speak a message of **wisdom** among the mature, but not the **wisdom** of this age or of the rulers of the age, who are coming to nothing. No, we speak of God's secret **wisdom**, a **wisdom** that has been hidden and that God destined for our glory before the world began." (I Corinthians 2:6-7)

Workman (Worker) - "As long as it is day, we must do the **work** of Him who sent me. Night is coming, when no one can **work**." (John 9:4) "As God's fellow **workers** we urge you not to receive God's grace in vain." (II Corinthians 6:1)"Do your best to present yourself to God as one approved, a **workman** who does not need to be ashamed and who correctly handles the word of truth." (II Timothy 2:15)

TEMPERANCE

For further study: Titus chapter 2

Temperance is basically self-control. It can be applied to refraining from the use of alcoholic beverages, controlling one's temper, or the avoidance of extreme outbursts in opinions, conduct, or feelings. It can also apply to constraints in eating and other personal behaviors. Galatians 5:23 tells us, "But the fruit of the Spirit is love, joy, peace, patience, kindness, goodness, faithfulness, gentleness, and self-control. Against such things there is no law." Christians must be under self-control in order to be an example and witness to the lost.

In speaking of the qualifications for an elder, Paul tells us, "An elder must be blameless, the husband of but one wife, a man whose children believe and are not open to the charge of being wild and disobedient. Since an overseer is entrusted with God's work, he must be blameless—not overbearing, not quick-tempered, not given to drunkenness, not violent, not pursuing dishonest gain. Rather he must be hospitable, one who loves what is good, who is self-controlled, upright, holy and disciplined." (Titus 1:6-8)

Abstinence - "He who regards one day special does so to the Lord. He who eats meat, eats to the Lord, for he gives thanks to God; and he who **abstains**, does so to the Lord and gives thanks to God." (Romans 14:6) "…I urge you, as aliens and strangers in the world, to **abstain** from sinful desires, which war against your soul." (I Peter 2:11)

Afflictions - "Be joyful in hope, patient in **affliction**, faithful in prayer." (Romans 12:12) "Now I rejoice in what was suffered for you and I fill up in my flesh what is still lacking in regard to Christ's **afflictions** for the sake of His body, which is the church."(Colossians 1:24)

Alertness - "No one knows about that day or hour, not even the angels in heave, nor the Son, but only the Father. Be on Guard! Be **alert**! You do not know when that time will come." (Mark 13:32-33) "Be self-controlled and **alert**. Your enemy the devil prowls around like a roaring lion looking for someone to devour." (I Peter 5:8)

Anger - "But now you must rid yourselves of all such things as these: **anger**, rage, malice, slander, and filthy language from your lips." (Colossians 3:8) My dear brothers, take note of this: Everyone should be quick to listen, slow to speak, and slow to become **angry**, for man's **anger** does not bring about the righteous life that God desires." (James 1:19-20)

Competence - "I myself am convinced, my brothers, that you yourselves are full of goodness, complete in knowledge and **competent** to instruct one another." (Romans 15:14) "Such confidence as this is ours through Christ before God. Not that we are **competent** in ourselves to claim anything for ourselves, but our **competence** comes from God. He has made us **competent** as ministers of a new covenant…." (II Corinthians 3:4-6)

Courage - "I eagerly expect and hope that I will in no way be ashamed, but will have sufficient **courage** so that now as always Christ will be exalted in by body, whether by life or by death." (Philippians 1:20) "But Christ is faithful as a Son over God's house. And we are His house, if we hold on to our **courage**…." (Hebrews 3:6)

Fellowship - "God, who has called you into **fellowship** with His Son Jesus Christ our Lord, is faithful." (I Corinthians 1:9) "But if we walk in the light, as He is in the light, we have **fellowship** with one another, and the blood of Jesus, His Son, purifies us from all sin." (I John 1:7)

Persecution - "Blessed are you when people insult you, **persecute** you and falsely say all kinds of evil against you because of me." (Matthew 5:11) "That is why, for Christ's sake, I delight in weaknesses, in insults, in hardships, in **persecutions**, in difficulties. For when I am weak, then I am strong." (II Corinthians 12:10)

Purification - "Since we have these promises, dear friends, let us **purify** ourselves from everything that contaminates body and spirit, perfecting holiness out of reverence for God." (II Corinthians 7:1) "Now that you have **purified** yourselves by obeying the truth so that you have sincere love for your brothers, love one another deeply, from the heart. (I Peter 1:22)

Renewing - "Do not conform any longer to the pattern of this world, but be transformed by the **renewing** of you mind." (Romans 12:2) "Do not lie to each other, since you have taken off your old self with its practices and have put on the **new self**, which is being **renewed** in knowledge in the image of its Creator." (Colossians 3:9-10)

Self-control - "But the fruit of the Spirit is love, joy, peace, patience, kindness, goodness, faithfulness, gentleness and **self-control**." (Galatians 5:22-23) "Therefore prepare your minds for action; be **self-controlled**; set your hope fully on the grace to be given you when Jesus Christ is revealed." (I Peter 1:13)

Service - "…prepare God's people for works of **service**, so that the body of Christ may be built up until we all reach unity in the faith and in the knowledge of the Son of God and become mature, attaining to the whole measure of the fullness of Christ." (Ephesians 4:12-13) "**Serve** wholeheartedly, as if you were **serving** the Lord, not men." (Ephesians 6:7)

Sexual immorality - "For out of the heart come evil thoughts, murder adultery, **sexual immorality**, theft, false testimony, slander. These are what make a man unclean…." (Matthew 15:19-20) "Flee from **sexual immorality**. All other sins a man commits are outside his body, but he who sins **sexually** sins against his own body." (I Corinthians 6:18)

Strength - "I can do everything through Him who gives me **strength**." (Philippians 4:13) "If anyone speaks, he should do it as one speaking the very words of God. If anyone serves, he should do it with the **strength** God provides, so that in all things God may be praised through Jesus Christ. To Him be the glory and the power forever and ever. Amen. (I Peter 4:11)

Suffering - "For it has been granted to you on behalf of Christ not only to believe on Him, but also to **suffer** for Him…." (Philippians 1:29) "For it is commendable if a man bears up under the pain of unjust **suffering** because he is conscious of God. But how is it to you credit if you receive a beating for doing wrong and endure it? But if you **suffer** for doing good and you endure it, this commendable before God. To this you were called, because Christ **suffered** for you, leaving you an example, that you should follow in His steps." (I Peter 2:19-21)

Temptation - "Watch and pray so that you will not fall into **temptation**. The spirit is willing, but the body is weak." (Matthew 26:41) "No **temptation** has seized you except what is common to man. And God if faithful; He will not let you be **tempted** beyond what you can bear. But when you are **tempted**, He will also provide a way out so that you can stand up under it." (I Corinthians 10:13)

The Body - "Do not offer parts of your **body** to sin, as instruments of wickedness, but rather offer yourselves to God, as those who have been brought from death to life; and offer the parts of your **body** to Him as instruments of righteousness, for sin shall not be your master, because you are not under law, but under grace." (Romans 6:13-14) "Do you not know that you **body** is a temple of the Holy Spirit, who is in you, whom you have received from God? You are not your own; you were bought at a price. Therefore honor God with your **body**." (I Corinthians 6:19)

Transformation - "Do not **conform** any longer to the pattern of this world, but be **transformed** by the renewing of your mind. Then you will be able to test and approve what God's will is – His good, pleasing, and perfect will." (Romans 12:2) "But our citizenship is in heaven. And we eagerly await a Savior from there, the Lord Jesus Christ, who, by the power that enables Him to bring everything under His control, will **transform** our lowly bodies so that they will be like His glorious body." (Philippians 3:20-21)

Trials - "Consider it pure joy, my brothers, whenever you face **trials** of many kinds, because you know that the testing of your faith develops perseverance." (James 1:2-3) "Blessed is the man who perseveres under **trial**, because when he has stood the test, he will receive the crown of life that God has promised to those who love Him." (James 1:12)

"and to temperance"

PATIENCE

For further study: James 5:7-12

"But they that wait upon the Lord shall renew their strength; they shall mount up with wings as eagles; they shall run, and not be weary; and they shall walk, and not faint." (Isaiah 40:31) (KJV) The Christian life is like running a marathon or completing a triathlon: one cannot run as if it is a hundred-yard dash. We have to run with patience so that we can endure and complete the whole race that God has set before us.

Paul encourages us by saying, "…work out your own salvation with fear and trembling. For it is God which worketh in you both to will and to do of His good pleasure." (Philippians 2:12-13) (KJV) Patience also brings its rewards to the believer: "We do not want you to become lazy, but to imitate those who through faith and patience inherit what has been promised." (Hebrews 6:12) In James we read, "Be patient, then, brothers, until the Lord's coming. See how the farmer waits for the land to yield its valuable crop and how patient he is for the autumn and spring rains." (James 5:7)

Affliction - "Be joyful in hope, patient in **affliction**, faithful in prayer." (Romans 12:12) "Now I rejoice in what was suffered for you, and I fill up in my flesh what is still lacking in regard to Christ's **afflictions**, for the sake of His body, which is the church." (Colossians 1:24)

Anxiety - "Cast all your **anxiety** on Him because He cares for you." (I Peter 5:7) "Do not be **anxious** about anything, but in everything, by prayer and petition, with thanksgiving, present you requests to God. And the peace of God, which transcends all understanding, will guard your hearts and you minds in Christ Jesus." (Philippians 4:6-7)

Burdens - "Come to me, all you who are weary and **burdened**, and I will give you rest. Take my yoke upon you and learn from me, for I am gentle and humble in heart, and you will find rest for your soul. For my yoke is easy and my **burden** is light." (Matthew 11:28-30) "Carry each other's **burdens**, and in this way you will fulfill the law of Christ." (Galatians 6:2)

Comfort - "My **comfort** in my suffering is this: Your promise preserves my life." (Psalm 119:50) "Praise be to the God and Father of our Lord Jesus Christ, the Father of compassion and the God of all **comfort**, who **comforts** us in all our troubles, so that we can **comfort** those in any trouble with the **comfort** we ourselves have received from God. For just as the sufferings of Christ flow over into our lives, so also through Christ our **comfort** overflows. If we are distressed, it is for your **comfort** and salvation; if we are **comforted**, it is for your **comfort** and salvation, which produces in you patient endurance of the same sufferings we suffer." (II Corinthians 1:3-6)

Consolation - "Now the God of patience and **consolation** grant you to be like-minded one toward another according to Christ Jesus." (Romans 15:5)(KJV)

Diligence - "You **diligently** study the Scriptures because you think that by them you possess eternal life. These are the Scriptures that testify about me." (John 5:39) "We want each of you to show this same **diligence** to the very end, in order to make your hope sure." (Hebrews 6:11)

Endurance - "If we are distressed, it is for your comfort and salvation; if we are comforted, it is for your comfort, which produces in you patient **endurance** of the same sufferings we suffer." (II Corinthians 1:6) "And we pray this in order that you may live a life worthy of the Lord and may please Him in every way: bearing fruit in every good work, growing in the knowledge of God, being strengthened with all power according to His glorious might so that you may have great **endurance** and patience, and joyfully giving thanks to the Father, who has qualified you to share in the inheritance of the saints in the kingdom of light." (Colossians 1:10-12)

Forbearance - "God presented Him as a sacrifice of atonement, through faith in His blood. He did this to demonstrate His justice, because in His **forbearance** He had left the sins committed beforehand unpunished—He did it to demonstrate His justice at the present time, so as to be just and the one who justifies those who have faith in Jesus." (Romans 3:25-26) "Be completely humble and gentle; be patient, **bearing** with one another in love. Make every effort to keep the unity of the Spirit through the bond of peace." (Ephesians 3:2-3)

God's patience - "Bear in mind that our **Lord's patience** means salvation, just as our dear brother Paul also wrote you with the wisdom that God gave him." (II Peter 3:15) "But for that very reason I was shown mercy so that in me, the worst of sinners, Christ Jesus might display **His** unlimited **patience** as an example for those who would believe on Him and receive eternal life." (I Timothy 1:16)

Great Worth - "These have come so that your faith—of **greater worth** than gold, which perishes even though refined by fire—may be proved genuine and may result in praise, glory and honor when Jesus Christ is revealed." (I Peter 1:7) "Instead it should be in your inner self, the unfading beauty of a gentle and quiet spirit, which is of **great worth** in God's sight." (I Peter 3:4)

Hardship - "Endure **hardship** with us like a good soldier of Jesus Christ." (II Timothy 2:3) "You have persevered and have endured **hardships** for my name, and have not grown weary." (Revelation 2:3)

Hope - "But if we **hope** for what we do not yet have, we wait for it patiently." (Romans 8:25) "We continually remember before our God and Father your work produced by faith, your labor prompter by love, and your endurance inspired by **hope** in our Lord Jesus Christ." (I Thessalonians 1:3)

Insults - "but He said to me, 'My grace is sufficient for you, for my power is made perfect in weakness. Therefore I will boast all the more gladly about my weaknesses, so that Christ's power may rest on me. That is why, for Christ's sake, I delight in weaknesses, in **insults**, in hardships, in persecutions, in difficulties, for when I am weak, then I am strong." (II Corinthians 12:9-10) "He committed no sin, and no deceit was found in His mouth. When they hurled their **insults** at Him, He did not retaliate; when He suffered, He made no threats...." (I Peter 2:22-23)

Longsuffering - "…walk worthy of the Lord unto all pleasing, being fruitful in every good work, and increasing in the knowledge of God; strengthened with all might, according to His glorious power, unto all patience and **longsuffering** with joyfulness…." (Colossians 1:11) (KJV)

Love - "**Love** is patient, love is kind. It does not envy, it does not boast, it is not proud." (I Corinthians 13:4) "Be completely humble and gentle; be patient, bearing with one another in **love**." (Ephesians 4:2)

Perseverance - "Consider it pure joy, my brothers, whenever you face trials of many kinds, because you know that the testing of your faith develops **perseverance. Perseverance** must finish its work so that you may be mature and complete, not lacking anything." (James 1:2-4) "As you know, we consider blessed those who have **persevered**. You have heard of Job's **perseverance** and have seen what the Lord finally brought about. The Lord is full of compassion and mercy." (James 5:11)

Promises - "We do not want you to become lazy, but to imitate those who through faith and patience inherit what has been **promised**." (Hebrews 6:12) "The Lord is not slow in keeping His **promise**, as some understand slowness; He is patient with you, not wanting anyone to perish, but everyone to come to repentance." (II Peter 3:9)

Quarrels - "A hot-tempered man stirs up dissension, but a patient man calms a **quarrel**." (Proverbs 15:18) "Don't have anything to do with foolish and stupid arguments, because you know that they produce **quarrels**." (II Timothy 2:23)

Quietness - "Make your ambition to lead a **quiet** life, to mind your own business and to work with your hands, just as we told you." (I Thessalonians 4:11) "Your beauty should not come from outward adornment, such as braided hair and the wearing of gold jewelry and fine clothes. Instead, it should be that of your inner self, the unfading beauty of a gentle and **quiet** spirit which is of great worth in God's sight." (I Peter 3:3-4)

Standing firm - "**Stand firm** then, with the belt of truth buckled around your waist, with the breastplate of righteousness in place, and with your feet fitted with the readiness that comes from the gospel of peace." (Ephesians 6:14-15) "You, too, be patient and **stand firm**, because the Lord's coming is near." (James 5:8)

Suffering - "Now if we are children, then we are heirs—heirs of God and co-heirs with Christ if indeed we share in His **sufferings** in order that we may also share in His glory." (Romans 8:17) "Brothers, as an example of patience in the face of **suffering**, take the prophets who spoke in the name of the Lord." (James 5:10)

Tribulation - "These things I have spoken unto you, that in me ye might have peace. In the world ye shall have **tribulation**; but be of good cheer; I have overcome the world." (John 16:33)(KJV) "…We glory in **tribulations** also: knowing that **tribulation** worketh patience; and patience, experience; and experience, hope…." (Romans 5:3-4) (KJV) (Revelation 7:15)

Understanding - "A patient man has great **understanding**, but a quick-tempered man displays folly." (Proverbs 14:29) "In Him we have redemption through His blood, the forgiveness of sins, in accordance with the riches of God's grace that He lavished on us will all wisdom and **understanding**." (Ephesians 1:7-8)

Wisdom - "A man's **wisdom** gives him patience; it is to his glory to overlook an offense." (Proverbs 19:11) "For I will give you words and **wisdom** that none of your adversaries will be able to resist or contradict." (Luke 21:15) "Bear in mind that our Lord's patience means salvation, just as our dear brother Paul also wrote you with the **wisdom** God gave him." (II Peter 3:15)

Waiting upon God - "Be still before the **Lord** and **wait** patiently for Him; do not fret when men succeed in their ways, when they carry out their wicked schemes." (Psalm 37:7-8) "…the Lord directs your hearts into the love of God, and into the patient **waiting for Christ**." (II Thessalonians 3:5) (KJV)

Worry - "Therefore I tell you, do not **worry** about your life, what you will eat or drink; or about your body, what you will wear…." (Matthew 6:25) "Who of you by **worrying** can add a single hour to his life?" (Matthew 6:27) "Therefore do not **worry** about tomorrow, for tomorrow will **worry** about itself. Each day has enough trouble of its own." (Matthew 6:34)

GODLINESS

For further study: I Peter 1:13-25; II Peter chapter 1

Paul encourages us to, "Make every effort to live in peace with all men and to be holy; without holiness no one will see the Lord." (Hebrews 12:14) We are also instructed, "But just as He who called you is holy, so be holy in all you do; for it is written: 'Be holy, because I am holy.'" (I Peter 1:15-16) Paul also tells us, "Since we have these promises, dear friends, let us purify ourselves from everything that contaminates body and spirit, perfecting holiness out of reverence for God." (II Corinthians 7:1) Therefore we know that godliness and holiness only come through the cleansing and purification of our lives that only God can give us. We cannot be godly and knowingly continue in our sinful ways.

Beauty of Holiness - "Give unto the Lord the glory due unto His name: bring an offering, and come before Him: worship the Lord in the **beauty of holiness**. (I Chronicles 16:29) (KJV) "...he appointed singers unto the Lord, and that should praise the **beauty of holiness**...." (II Chronicles 20:21) (KJV)

Baptism of the Holy Spirit - "I **baptize** you with water for repentance. But after me will come one who is more powerful than I, whose sandals I am not fit to carry. He will **baptize** you with **the Holy Spirit** and with fire." (Matthew 3:11) "Peter replied, 'Repent and be **baptized**, every one of you, in the name of Jesus Christ for the forgiveness of your wins. And you will receive the gift of **the Holy Spirit**.' " (Acts 2:38)

Behavior - "The aged women likewise, that they be in **behavior** as becometh holiness, not false accusers, not given to much wine, teachers of good things." (Titus 2:3)(KJV) "Let us **behave** decently, as in the daytime, not in orgies and drunkenness, not in sexual immorality and debauchery, not in dissension and jealousy. Rather, clothe yourselves with the Lord Jesus Christ, and do not think about how to gratify the desires of the sinful nature." (Romans 13:13-14) "But in your hearts set apart Christ as Lord. Always be prepared to give an answer to everyone who asks you to give the reason for the hope that you have. But do this with gentleness and respect, keeping a clear conscience so that those who speak maliciously against you good **behavior** in Christ may be ashamed of their slander." (I Peter 3:15-16)

Blameless - "May He (Jesus) strengthen your hears so that you will be **blameless** and holy in the presence of our God and Father when our Lord Jesus comes with all His holy ones." (I Thessalonians 3:13) "May God Himself, the God of peace, sanctify you through and through. May your whole spirit, soul and body, be kept **blameless** at the coming of our Lord Jesus Christ. The one who calls you is faithful and He will do it." (I Thessalonians 5:23-24)

Consecration - "For the law maketh men high priests which have infirmity; but the word of the oath, which was since the law, maketh the Son, who is **consecrated** for evermore." (Hebrews 7:28)(KJV) "And their sins and iniquities will I remember no more. Now where remission of these is, there is no more offering for sin. Having therefore, brethren, boldness to enter into the holiest by the blood of Jesus, by a new and living way, which He hath **consecrated** for us, through veil, that is to say, His flesh…."(Hebrews 10:17-20)(KJV)

Contentment - "…I have learned to be **content** whatever the circumstances." (Philippians 4:11) "But godliness with **contentment** is great gain. For we brought nothing into the world, and we can take nothing out of it. But if we have food and clothing, we will be **content** with that. People who want to get rich fall into temptation and a trap and into many foolish and harmful desires that plunge men into ruin and destruction." (I Timothy 6:6-9)

Conversation (Speech) - "Let your **conversation** be always full of grace, seasoned with salt, so that you may know how to answer everyone."

(Colossians 4:6) "Don't let anyone look down on you because you are young, but set an example for the believers in **speech**, in life, in love, in faith and in purity." (I Timothy 4:12) "Whoever would love life and see good days must keep his tongue from evil and his lips from deceitful **speech**." (I Peter 3:10)

Devine Nature - "For since the creation of the world God's invisible qualities—His eternal power and **divine nature**—have been clearly seen, being understood from what has been made, so that men are without excuse." (Romans 1:20) "Through these He has given us His very great and precious promises, so that through them, you may participate in the **divine nature** and escape the corruption in the world caused by evil desires." (II Peter 1:4)

Divine Power - "The weapons we fight with are not the weapons of the world. On the contrary, they have **divine power** to demolish strongholds. We demolish arguments and every pretension that sets itself up against the knowledge of God, and we take captive every thought to make it obedient to Christ. And we will be ready to punish every act of disobedience, once your obedience is complete." (II Corinthians 10:4-6) "His **divine power** has given us everything we need for life and godliness through our knowledge of Him who called us by His own glory and goodness. (II Peter 1:3)

Devotion - "This is a trustworthy saying. And I want you to stress these things, so that those who have trusted in God may be careful to **devote** themselves to doing what is good. These things are excellent and profitable for everyone." (Titus 3:8) "I am saying this for your own good, not to restrict you, but that you may live in a right way in undivided **devotion** to the Lord." (I Corinthians 7:35)

Doctrine - "Jesus answered them, and said, 'My **doctrine** is not mine, but His that sent me. If any man will do His will, he shall know of the **doctrine**, whether it be of God, or whether I speak of myself.' " (John 7:16-17) (KJV) "Watch your life and **doctrine** closely. Persevere in them, because if you do, you will save both yourself and your hearers." (I Timothy 4:16)

Exercise - "... **exercise** thyself rather unto godliness." (I Timothy 4:7) (KJV)

Gifts - "…I remind you to fan into flame the **gift** of God, which is in you trough the laying on of my hands. For God did not give us a spirit of timidity, but a spirit of power, of love and of self-discipline." (II Timothy 1:6-7) "…Since you are eager to have spiritual **gifts**, try to excel in **gifts** that build up the church." (I Corinthians 14:12)

Glory - "…Jesus said, 'This sickness will not end in death. No, it is for God's **glory** so that God's Son may be **glorified** through it.'" (John 11:4) "His divine power has given us everything we need for life and godliness through our knowledge of Him who called us by His own **glory** and goodness." (II Peter 1: 3)

Holiness - "But now that you have been set free from sin and have become slaves to God, the benefit you reap leads to **holiness**, and the result is eternal life. For the wages of sin is death, but the gift of God is eternal life in Christ Jesus our Lord." (Romans 6:22-23) "…God disciplines us for our good that we may share in His **holiness**." (Hebrews 12:10)

Holy Spirit (Holy Ghost) - "Anyone who speaks a word against the Son of Man will be forgiven, but anyone who speaks against the **Holy Spirit** will not be forgiven, either in this age or in the age to come." (Matthew 12:32) "I baptize you with water, but He will baptize you with the **Holy Spirit**." (Mark 1:8) "And do not grieve the **Holy Spirit** of God, with whom you were sealed for the day of redemption." (Ephesians 6:30)

Honesty - "Do not use **dishonest** standards when measuring length, weight or quantity. Use **honest** scales and **honest** weights, an **honest** ephah and an **honest** hin." (Leviticus 19:35-36) "Recompense to no man evil for evil. Provide things **honest** in the sight of all men." (Romans 12:17) (KJV) "I exhort therefore, that, first intercessions, and giving of thanks, be made for all men; for kings and for all that are in authority; that we may lead a quiet and peaceable life in all godliness and **honesty**." (I Timothy 2:1-2)(HJV)

Mystery - "My purpose is that they may be encouraged in heart and united in love, so that they may have the full riches of complete understand, in order that they may know the **mystery** of God, namely, Christ." (Colossians 2:2) "Beyond all question, the **mystery** of godliness is great: He appeared in a body, was vindicated by the spirit, was seen by angels, was preached among the nations, was believed on in the world, was taken up in glory." (I Timothy 3:16)

Pentecost - "When the day of **Pentecost** came, they were all together in one place. Suddenly a sound like the blowing of a violent wind came from heaven and filled the whole house where they were sitting. They saw what seemed to be tongues of fire that separated and came to rest on each of them. All of them were filled with the Holy Spirit and began to speak in other tongues as the Spirit enabled them." (Acts 2:1-4)

Perfection of holiness - "Since we have these promises, dear friends, let us purify ourselves from everything that contaminates body and spirit, **perfecting holiness** out of reverence for God." (II Corinthians 7:1)

Profitability - "This is a trustworthy saying. And I want you to stress these things, so that those who have trusted in God may be careful to devote themselves to doing what is good. These things are excellent and **profitable** for everyone." (I Timothy (4:8)

Purification - "The Son is the radiance of God's glory and the exact representation of His being, sustaining all things by His powerful word. After he had provided **purification** for sins, He sat down at the right hand of the Majesty in heaven. (Hebrews 1:3) "Since we have these promises, dear friends, let us **purify** ourselves from everything that contaminates body and spirit, perfecting holiness out of reverence for God." (II Corinthians 7:1)

Reverence - "Therefore, since we are receiving a kingdom that cannot be shaken, let us be thankful, and so worship God acceptably with **reverence** and awe, for our God is a consuming fire." (Hebrews 12:28) "Submit to one another out of **reverence** for Christ." (Ephesians 5:21)

Righteousness - "For in the gospel a **righteousness** from God is revealed, a **righteousness** that is by faith from first to last, just as it is written: 'The **righteous** will live by faith.' " (Luke 1:75) "You were taught, with regard to your former way of life, to put off your old self, which is being corrupted by its deceitful desires; to be made new in the attitude of you minds; and to put on the new self, created to be like God in true **righteousness** and holiness." (Ephesians 4:22-24)

Sabbath-rest - "Then they went home and prepared spices and perfumes. But they **rested** on the **Sabbath** in obedience to the commandment." (Luke 23:56) "There remains, then, a **Sabbath-rest** for the people of God;

for anyone who enters God's **rest** also **rests** from his own work, just as God did from His." (Hebrews 4:9)

Sacredness - "Do not give to dogs that which is **sacred**; do not throw you pearls to pigs. If you do, they may trample them under their feet, and then turn and tear you to pieces." (Matthew 7:6) "If anyone destroys God's temple, God will destroy him; for God's temple is **sacred**, and you are that temple." (I Corinthians 3:17)

Sanctification - "May God Himself, the God of Peace, **sanctify** you through and through. May your whole spirit, soul and body be kept blameless at the coming of our Lord Jesus Christ." (I Thessalonians 5:23) "But we ought always to thank God for you, brothers loved by the Lord, because from the beginning God chose you to be saved through the **sanctifying** work of the Spirit and through belief in the truth." (II Thessalonians 2:13)

Spirit - " 'In the last days,' God says, 'I will pour out my **Spirit** on all people. Your sons and daughters will prophesy, your young men will see visions, your old men will dream dreams. Even on my servants, both men and women, I will pour out my **Spirit** in those days, and they will prophesy.' " (Acts 2:17) "…regarding His Son, who as to His human nature was a descendant of David, and who through the **Spirit** of holiness was declared with power to be the Son of God by His resurrection from the deaf: Jesus Christ our Lord." (Romans 1:3-4)

Truth - "…we have renounced secret and shameful ways; we do not use deception, nor do we distort the Word of God. On the contrary, by setting forth the **truth** plainly we commend ourselves to every man's conscience in the sight of God." (II Corinthians 2:2) "Paul, a servant of God and an apostle of Jesus Christ for the faith of God's elect and the knowledge of the **truth** that leads to godliness--…."

Worship - "Therefore, I urge you, brothers, in view of God's mercy, to offer you bodies as living sacrifices, holy and pleasing to God—this is your spiritual act of **worship**." (Romans 12:1) "**Worship** the Lord in the splendor of His holiness; tremble before Him, all the earth."(Psalm 96:9)

BROTHERLY KINDNESS

For further study: Luke chapter 10

In Ephesians we are encouraged to, "Be kind and compassionate to one another, forgiving each other, just as in Christ God forgave you." (Ephesians 4:32) God expects us to take on the same traits toward one another that He, through Jesus Christ, has already displayed to all mankind. In

I Thessalonians 4:6 we read, "...no one should wrong his brother or take advantage of him. The Lord will punish men for all such sins, as we have already told you and warned you." Therefore, we know that God does hold us accountable for how we treat each other once we become Christians. We are warned, "Anyone who claims to be in the light but hates his brother is still in darkness." (I John 2:9) Throughout the New Testament, Christians called one another brothers and sisters in Christ.

Jesus, in speaking to Peter before His crucifixion asked, "Simon son of John, do you love me?" and Peter answered, "Yes, Lord, you know that I love you." Jesus then concluded, "Take care of my sheep." (John 21:16

In the story of the Good Samaritan, a legal expert asked Jesus what he must do to inherit eternal life. When asked what the law instructed, the man replied, "Love the Lord your God with all your heart and with all you soul and with all your strength and with all your mind," and "Love your neighbor as yourself." After confirming to the man that he had answered correctly, the man wanted to justify himself by asking, "And who is my neighbor?" After telling the story of the traveler from Jericho who fell among thieves and how two men, a priest and a Levite, ignored the wounded man, and a third, a despised Samaritan did all he could to help him, Jesus asked the man of the law, "Which of these three do think was a neighbor to the man who fell into the hands of robbers?" The man correctly answered, "The one who had mercy on him." Jesus then told the man to do the same thing for others. (Luke 10:25-37)

Aid - "Yet it was good of you to share in my troubles. Moreover, as you Philippians know, in the early days of your acquaintance with the gospel, when I set out from Macedonia, not one church shared with me in the matter of giving and receiving, except you only; for even when I was in Thessalonica, you sent me **aid** again and again when I was in need." (Philippians 4:14-16)

Benevolence - "Let the husband render unto his wife due **benevolence**: and likewise also the wife unto the husband." (I Corinthians 7:3)(KJV)

Brotherly love - "Be devoted to one another in **brotherly love**. Honor one another above yourselves.

(Romans 12:10) "Now about **brotherly love** we do not need to write to you, for you yourselves have been taught by God to **love** each other. And in fact, you do **love** all the **brothers** throughout Macedonia. Yet we urge you, **brothers**, to do so more and more." (I Thessalonians 4:9-10)

Burdens - "Come to me, all you who are weary and **burdened**, and I will give you rest. Take my yoke upon you and learn from me, for I am gentle and humble in heart, and you find rest for your souls. For my yoke is easy and my **burden** is light." (Matthew 11:28-30) "Carry each other's **burdens**, and in this way you will fulfill the law of Christ." (Galatians 6:2)

Care - "After all, no one ever hated his own body, but he feeds and cares for it, just as Christ does the church." (Ephesians 5:29) "Be shepherds of God's flock that is under you **care**, serving as overseers—not because you must, but because you are willing, as God wants you to be; not greedy for money, but eager to serve." (I Peter 5:2)

Comfort - "Praise be to the God and Father of our Lord Jesus Christ, the Father of compassion and the God of all **comfort**, who **comforts** us in all our troubles, so that we can **comfort** those in any trouble with the **comfort** we ourselves have received from God. For just as the sufferings of Christ flow over into our lives, so also through Christ our **comfort** overflows. If we are distressed, it is for you **comfort** and salvation; if we are **comforted**, it is for your **comfort** which produce in you patient endurance of the same sufferings we suffer. And our hope for you is firm, because we know that just as you share in our sufferings, so also you share in our **comfort**." (II Corinthians 1:3-7)

Compassion - "Be kind and **compassionate** to one another, forgiving each other, just as in Christ God forgave you." (Ephesians 4:32) "Therefore, as God's chosen people, holy and dearly loved, clothe yourselves with **compassion**, kindness, humility, gentleness, and patience." (Colossians 3:12)

Concern - "...There should be no division in the body, but that its parts should have equal **concern** for each other. If one part suffers, every part suffers with it; it one part is honored, every part rejoices with it." (I Corinthians 12:25-26) "See what this godly sorrow has produced in you: what earnestness, what eagerness to clear yourselves, what indignation, what alarm, what longing, what **concern**, what readiness to see justice done...." (II Corinthians 7:11)

Consideration - "**Consider** therefore the kindness and sternness of God: sternness to those who fell, but kindness to you, provided that you continue in His kindness. Otherwise, you also will be cut off." (Romans 11:22) "Remind the people to be subject to rulers and authorities, to be obedient, to be ready to do whatever is good, to slander no one, to be peaceable and **considerate**, and to show true humility toward all men." (Titus 3:1-2)

Edification - "Let us therefore make every effort to do what leads to peace and to mutual **edification**." (Romans 14:19) "He who speaks in a tongue **edifies** himself, but he who prophesies **edifies** the church. I would like every one of you to speak in tongues, but I would rather have you prophesy. He who prophesies is greater than one who speaks in tongues, unless he interprets, so that the church may be **edified**." (I Corinthians 14:4-5)(KJV)

Encouragement - "I long to see you so that I may impart to you some spiritual gift to make you strong—that is, that you and I may be mutually **encouraged** by each other's faith." (Romans 1:11-12) "...each member belongs to all the others. We have different gifts, according to the grace given us....If it is **encouraging**, let him **encourage**...." (Romans 12:6-8)

Example - "Don't let anyone look down on you because you are young, but set an **example** for the believers in speech, in life, in love, in faith, and in purity." (I Timothy 4:12) "To this you were called, because Christ suffered for you, leaving you an **example**, that you should follow in His steps." (I Peter 2:21)

Forgiveness - "**Forgive** us our debts, as we also have **forgiven** our debtors. And lead us not into temptation, but deliver us from the evil one. For if you **forgive** men when they sin against you, your heavenly Father will also **forgive** you. But if you do not **forgive** men their sins, your Father will not **forgive** your sins." (Matthew 6:12-15) "Bear with each other and **forgive** whatever grievances you may have against one another. **Forgive** as the Lord **forgave** you." (Colossians 3:13)

Gentleness - "Let your **gentleness** be evident to all. The Lord is near." (Philippians 4:5) "But in your hearts set apart Christ as Lord. Always be prepared to give an answer to everyone who asks you to give the reason for the hope that you have. But do this with **gentleness** and respect." (I Peter 3:15)

Giving - "But just as you excel in everything—in faith, in speech, in knowledge, in complete earnestness and in your love for us—see that you also excel in this grace of **giving**." (II Corinthians 8:6-7) "Remember this: Whoever sows sparingly will also reap sparingly, and whoever sows generously will also reap generously. Each man should **give** what he has decided in his heart to **give**, not reluctantly or under compulsion, for God loves a cheerful **giver**." (II Corinthians 9:6-7)

Helping - "In everything I did, I showed you that by this kind of hard work we must **help** the weak, remembering the words the Lord Jesus Himself said: 'It is more blessed to give than to receive.' " (Acts 20:35) "… the Spirit helps us in our weakness…." (Romans 8:26) "God is not unjust; He will not forget your work and the love you have shown Him as you have helped His people and continue to help them." (Hebrews 6:10)

Hospitality - "Share with God's people who are in need. Practice **hospitality**." (Romans 12:13) "Offer **hospitality** to one another without grumbling." (I Peter 4:9)

Humility (Humbleness) - "Do nothing out of selfish ambition or vain conceit, but in **humility** consider others better than yourselves."

(Philippians 3:2) "Who is wise and understanding among you? Let him show it by his good life, by deeds don in the **humility** that comes from wisdom." (James 3:13)

Interests - "Each of you should look not only unto your own **interests**, but also to the **interests** of others." (Philippians 2:4) "I have no one else like him (Timothy), who takes a genuine **interest** in your welfare. For everyone looks out for his own **interests**, not those of Jesus Christ. (Philippians 2:20-21)

Kindness - "Or do you show contempt for the riches of His **kindness**, tolerance, and patience, not realizing that God's **kindness** leads you toward repentance?" (Romans 2:4) "Consider therefore the **kindness** and sternness of God: sternness to those who fell, but **kindness** to you, provided that you continue in His **kindness**. Otherwise, you also will be cut off." (Romans 11:22)

Respect - "Now we ask you, brothers, to **respect** those who work hard among you, who are over you in the Lord and who admonish you. Hold them in the highest regard in love because of their work. Live in peace with each other." (I Thessalonians 5:12) "Show proper **respect** to everyone: Love the brotherhood of believers, fear God, honor the king." (I Peter 2:17)

Sharing - "This service that you perform is not only <u>supplying the needs of God's people</u> but is also overflowing in many expressions of thanks to God. Because of the service by which you have proved yourselves, men will praise God for the obedience that accompanies your confession of the gospel of Christ, and for your generosity in **sharing** with them and with everyone else." (II Corinthians 9:12-13)

The Needy - "Be careful not to do you 'acts of righteousness' before men, to be seen by them. If you do, you will have no reward from your Father in heaven. So when you give to **the needy**, do not announce it with trumpets, as the hypocrites do in the synagogues and on the streets, to be honored by men..., but when you give to **the needy**, do not let your left hand know what your right hand is doing, so that your giving may be in secret. Then your Father, who sees what is done in secret, will reward you." (Matthew 6:1-4) "For I was hungry and you gave Me something to eat, I was thirsty and you gave Me something to drink, I was a stranger and you invited Me in, I **needed** clothes and you clothed Me, I was sick and you looked after Me, I was in prison and you came to visit Me. Then the righteous will answer Him, 'Lord, when did we see You hungry and feed You, or thirsty and give You something to drink? When did we see You a stranger and invite You in, or **needing** clothes and clothe You? When did we see You sick or in prison and go to visit You?' The King will reply, 'I tell you the truth, whatever you did for the one of the least of these brothers of mine, you did for Me.' " (Matthew 26:35-46)

Zeal - "Those people are **zealous** to win you over, but for no good. What they want is to alienate you from us, so that you may be **zealous** for them. It is fine to be **zealous**, provided the purpose is good, and to be so always and not just when I am with you." (Galatians 4:17-18)

LOVE

For further study: I Corinthians chapter 13; I John chapter 4

Love is one of the most-often mentioned words in the Bible, yet, in our human weaknesses, it is probably the most difficult to follow. Jesus said, "A new commandment I give you: Love one another. As I have loved you, so must you love one another." (John 13:34) Just as there are degrees of faith, there are also degrees of love. Jesus said, "Greater love has no one than this, that he lay down his life for his friends." (John 15:13) In the following verses, He also said that we are His friends and commanded that we love each other. In Corinthians Paul tells us, "And now I will show you the most excellent way. If I speak in the tongues of men and of angels, but have not love, I am only a resounding gong or a clanging cymbal." (I Corinthians 12:31-13:1) Jesus warns us, "But I tell you: Love your enemies and pray for those who persecute you, that you may be sons of your Father in heaven…." (Matthew 5:44-45) John tells us, "And so we know and rely on the love God has for us. God is love. Whoever lives in love lives in God, and God in him…There is no fear in love. But perfect love drives out fear, because fear has to do with punishment. The one who fears is not made perfect in love…And He has given us this command: "Whoever loves God must also love his brother." (I John 4:16-21)

Affection - "And his (Titus') **affection** for you is all the greater when he remembers that you were all obedient, receiving him with fear and trembling." (II Corinthians 7:15) "God can testify how I long for all of you with the **affection** of Christ Jesus." (Philippians 1:8)

Atonement - "God presented Him as a sacrifice of atonement, through faith in His blood. He did this to demonstrate His justice because in His forbearance He had left the sins committed beforehand unpunished…." (Romans 3:25) "This is love: not that we loved God, but that He loved us and sent his Son as an **atoning** sacrifice for our sins." (I John 4:10)

Book of Life – "He who overcomes will like, them, be dressed in white. I will never blot out his name from the **book of life**, but will acknowledge his name before my Father and His angels." (Revelation 3:5) "And I saw the dead, great and small, standing before the throne, and **books** were opened. Another **book** was opened, which is the **book of life**. The dead were judged according to what they had done as recorded in the **books**." (Revelation 20:12)

Charity - "Though I speak with the tongues of men and of angels, and have not **charity**, I am become as sounding brass, or a tinkling cymbal. And though I have the gift of prophecy, and understand all mysteries, and all knowledge; and though I have all faith, so that I could remove mountains, and have not **charity**, I am nothing." (I Corinthians 13:1-2) (KJV) "And above all these things put on **charity**, which is the bond of perfectness." (Colossians 3:14)(KJV)

Commands (Commandments) - "One of them, an expert in the law, tested Him with this question: 'Teacher, which is the greatest **commandment** in the Law?' Jesus replied, 'Love the Lord you God with all your heart and with all you soul and with all your mind.' This is the first and greatest commandment. And the second is like it: 'Love your neighbor as yourself.' All the Law and Prophets hang on these two **commandments**." (Matthew 22:35-40) "My **command** is this: Love each other as I have loved you. Greater love has no one than this, that he lay down his life for his friends." (John 15:12-13)

Compassion - "Filled with **compassion**, Jesus reached out His hand and touched them. 'I am willing,' He said. 'Be clean.' " (Mark 1:41) "If you have any encouragement from being united with Christ, if any comfort from His love, if any fellowship with the Spirit, if any tenderness and **compassion**, then make my joy complete by being like-minded, having the same love, being one in spirit and purpose." (Philippians 2:1-2)

Debt - "Let no **debt** remain outstanding, except the continuing **debt** to love one another, for he who loves his fellow man has fulfilled the law." (Romans 13:8)

Enemies - "You have heard that it was said, 'Love your neighbor and hate your **enemy**.' But I tell you: Love your **enemies** and pray for those who persecute you that you may be sons of your Father in heaven...." (Matthew 5:43-45) "But love your **enemies**, do good to them, and lend to them without expecting to get anything back. Then your reward will be great, and you will be sons of the Most High, because He is kind to the ungrateful and wicked." (Luke 6:35)

Fear - "There is no **fear** in love. But perfect love drives out **fear**, because **fear** has to do with punishment. The one who **fears** is not made perfect in love." (I John 4:8)

Fulfillment - "Let no debt remain outstanding, except the continuing debt to love one another, for he who loves his fellow man has **fulfilled** the law.... whatever other commandment there may be, are summed up in this one rule: Love you neighbor as yourself. Love does no harm to its neighbor. Therefore love is the **fulfillment** of the law." (Romans 13:8-10)

Giving - "For God so loved the world that He **gave** His one and only Son, that whoever believes in Him shall not perish but have eternal life." (John 3:16) "But just as you excel in everything—in faith, in speech, in knowledge, in complete earnestness and in your love for us—see that you also excel in this grace of **giving**." (II Corinthians 8:7)

God - "**God** is love. Whoever lives in love lives in **God**, and **God** in him. In this way love is made complete among us so that we will have confidence on the Day of Judgment, because in this world we are like Him." (I John 4:16-17) "But **God** demonstrates His own love for us in this: While we were yet sinners, Christ died for us." (Romans 5:8)

Greatest Love - "**Greater love** has no one that this, that he lay down his life for his friends." (John 15:13)

Heart - "The goal of this command is love, which comes from a pure **heart** and a good conscience and a sincere faith." (I Timothy 1:5) "Now that you have purified yourselves by obeying the truth so that you have sincere love for your brothers, love one another deeply from the **heart**." (I Peter 1:22)

Jesus' Love - "It was just before the Passover Feast. **Jesus** knew that the time had come for Him to leave this world and go to the Father. Having **loved** His own who were in the world, He now showed them the full extent of **His love**. (John 13:1) "This is how we know what **love** is: **Jesus Christ** laid down His life for us, and we ought to lay down our lives for our brothers." (I John 3:16)

Neighbors - "...love your **neighbor** as yourself." (Matthew 19:19) "The entire law is summed up in a single command: 'Love your **neighbor** as yourself." (Galatians 5:14)

Never Failing - "Love **never fails**. But where there are prophecies, they will cease; where there are tongues, they will be stilled; where there is knowledge, it will pass away." (I Corinthians 13:8)

Obedience - "Whoever has my commands and **obeys** them, he is the one who loves me. He who loves me will be loved by my Father, and I too will hove him and show myself to him." (John 14:21) "And this is love: that we walk in **obedience** to His commands. As you have heard from the beginning, His command is that you walk in love." (II John 6)

Patient and Kind - "Love is **patient**. Love is **kind**. It does not envy, it does not boast, it is not proud." (I Corinthians 13:4) "But the fruit of the Spirit is love, joy, peace patience, **kindness**, goodness, faithfulness, gentleness and self-control. Against such things there is no law." (Galatians 5:22-23) "Be completely humble and gentle; be **patient**, bearing one another in love." (Ephesians 4:2)

Perfection - "...Aim for **perfection**, listen to my appeal, be of one mind, live in peace. And the God of love and peace sill be with you." (II Corinthians 13:11) "There is no fear in love. But **perfect** love drives out fear, because fear has to do with punishment. The one who fears is not made **perfect** in love. We love because He first loved us." (I John 4:18-19)

Perseverance - "Blessed is the man who **perseveres** under trial, because when he has stood the test, he will receive the crown of life that God has promised to those who love Him." (James 1:12) "May the Lord direct your hearts into God's love and Christ's perseverance." (II Thessalonians 3:5)

Rewards – "For the Son of Man is going to come in His Father's glory with His angels, and then He will **reward** each person according to what he has done." (Matthew 16:27) "I tell you the truth, anyone who gives you a cup of water in my name because you belong to Christ will certainly not lose his **reward**." (Mark 9:41)

Sacrifice - "Be imitators of God, therefore, as dearly loved children and live a life of love, just as Christ loved us and gave Himself up for us as a fragrant offering and **sacrifice** to God." (Ephesians 5:1-2) "This is love: not that we loved God, but that He loved us and sent His Son as an atoning **sacrifice** for our sins." (I John 4:10)

Sincerity - "Love must be **sincere**. Hate what is evil; cling to what is good." (Romans 12:9) "I am not commanding you, but I want to test the **sincerity** of your love by comparing it with the earnestness of others." (II Corinthians 8:8) "The goal of this command is love, which comes from a pure heart and a good conscience and a **sincere** faith." (I Timothy 1:5)

Tenderness - "If you have any encouragement from being united with Christ, if any comfort from His love, if any fellowship with the Spirit, if any **tenderness** and compassion, then make my joy complete by being like-minded, having the same love, being one in spirit and purpose." (Philippians 2:1-2)

Unity - "My purpose is that they may be encouraged in heart and **united** in love, so that they may have the full riches of complete understanding, in order that they may know the mystery of God, , namely, Christ, in whom are hidden all the treasures of wisdom and knowledge." (Colossians 2:2-3) "And over all these virtues put on love, which binds them all together in perfect **unity**." (Colossians 3:14)

Virtue - "Over all these **virtues** put on love, which bind them together in perfect unity." (Colossians 3:14)

Worldly Love - "Do not **love the world** or anything in the **world**. If anyone **loves the world**, the **love** of the Father is not in him. Fir everything in the **world**—the cravings of the sinful men, the lust of his eyes and the boasting of what he has and does—comes not from the Father but from the **world**. The **world** and its desires pass away, but the man who does the will of God lives forever.'" (I John 2:15-17)

PART II

<hr>

MAN'S BYWAY

Unbelief

For further study: Romans Chapters 6-8

Being a retired school teacher, I know that many students lose things which are very valuable to them, but many of these items languish in the Lost and Found, never to be claimed by their rightful owners. How much more so do people not claim what God has promised to them: eternal life though the sacrifice that Jesus Christ made on the cross to save them from their sins. His promise is the most valuable possession of all: eternal life; but so often we do not claim what if rightfully ours through His promises.

Matthew records the words of Jesus and tells us what will happen when Jesus Christ returns to the earth. Jesus told His disciples, "When the Son of Man comes in His glory, and all the angels with Him, He will sit on His throne in heavenly glory. All the nations will be gathered before Him, and He will separate the people one from another as a shepherd separates the sheep from the goats. He will put the sheep on His right and the goats on His left." (Matthew 25:31-33) What is the deciding factor that Christ will use in this separation? It is faith in the Lord Jesus Christ. "Without faith it is impossible to please God." (Hebrews 11:6) "But what does it (the Scripture) say? 'The word is near you; it is in your mouth and in your heart, that is, the word of faith we are proclaiming: That if you confess with your mouth, 'Jesus is Lord,' and believe in your heart that God raised Him from the dead, you will be saved. For it is with your heart that you believe and are justified, and it is with your mouth that you confess and are saved.' As the Scripture says, 'Anyone who trusts in Him will never be put to shame.' " (Romans 10:8-11) There are many things that Satan puts into this world and peoples' hearts that prevent them from coming to a saving knowledge of Jesus Christ. We are warned, "Be self-controlled and alert. Your enemy the devil prowls around like a roaring lion looking for someone to devour.

Resist him, standing firm in the faith, because you know that your brothers throughout the world are undergoing the same kind of sufferings." (I Peter 5:8-9) There are many who will not enter into the Kingdom of Heaven because they do not believe that Jesus is our Lord and Savior. There are many factors which interfere with their willingness to believe.

Blasphemy – "And so I tell you, every sin and **blasphemy** will be forgiven men, but the **blasphemy** against the Spirit will not be forgiven. Anyone who speaks a word against the Son of Man will be forgiven, but anyone who speaks against the Holy Spirit will not be forgiven, either in this age or in the age to come." (Matthew 12:31-32) "I tell you the truth, all the sins and **blasphemies** of men will be forgiven them. But whoever **blasphemes** against the Holy Spirit will never be forgiven; he is guilty of an eternal sin." (Mark 3:28-29)

Condemnation – "…whoever does not **believe** will be **condemned**." (Mark 16:16)

Conforming – "Do not **conform** any longer to the pattern of this world…." (Romans 12:2) "As obedient children, do not **conform** to the evil desires that you had when you lived in ignorance." (I Peter 1:14)

Corruption – "Do not be misled: 'Bad company **corrupts** good character.' " (I Corinthians 15:33) "To the pure, all things are pure, but to those who are **corrupted** and do not believe, nothing is pure. In fact, both their minds and consciences are **corrupted**." (Titus 1:15) "The tongue also is a fire, a world of evil among the parts of the body. It **corrupts** the whole person, sets the whole course of his life on fire, and is itself set on fire by hell." (James 3:6)

Cunning – "Just as Eve was deceived by the serpent's **cunning**, our minds may somehow be led astray from your sincere and pure devotion to Christ." (II Corinthians 11:3) "Then we will no longer be infants, tossed back and forth by the waves, and blown here and there by every wind of teaching and by the **cunning** and craftiness of men in their deceitful scheming." (Ephesians 4:14)

Darkness – "But if your eyes are bad, your whole body will be full of **darkness**. If then the light within you is **darkness**, how great is that

darkness. (Matthew 6:23) "The light shines in the **darkness**, but the **darkness** has not understood it." (John 1:5) "This is the verdict: Light has come into the world, but men loved **darkness** instead of light because their deeds were evil. (John 3:19)

Death – "What benefit did you reap at that time from the things you are now ashamed of? Those things result in **death**!...For the wages of sin is **death**...." (Romans 6:21-23) "What a wretched man I am! Who will rescue me from this body of death?" (Romans 7:24)

Denial – "...without love, unforgiving, slanderous, without self control, brutal, not lovers of the good, treacherous, rash conceited, lovers of pleasure rather than lovers of God—having a form of godliness but **denying** its power. Have nothing to do with them." (II Timothy 3:3-5) "They claim to know God, but by their actions they **deny** Him...." (Titus 1:16)

Disbelief – "For John came to you to show you the way of righteousness, and you did **not believe** him, but the tax collectors and the prostitutes did. And even after you say this, you did **not** repent and **believe** him." (Matthew 21:32) "Whoever **believes** and is baptized will be saved, but whoever does not **believe** will be condemned." (Mark 16:16) "Those along the path are the ones who hear, and then the devil comes and takes away the word from their hearts, so that they may **not believe** and be saved." (Luke 8:12) "I told you that you would die in your sins; if you do **not believe** that I am the one I claim to be, you will indeed die in your sins." (John 8:24)

Disobedience – "It still remains that some will enter that rest, and those who formerly had the gospel preached to them did not go in, because of their **disobedience**." (Hebrews 4:6) "Let no one deceive you with empty words, for because of such things God's wrath comes on those who are **disobedient**." (Ephesians 5:6) "People will be lovers of themselves, lovers of money, boastful, proud, abusive, **disobedient** to the parents...." (II Timothy 3:2) "They claim to know God, but by their actions they deny Him. They are detestable, **disobedient** and unfit for doing anything good." (Titus 1:16)

Doubt – "Then He said to Thomas, 'put your finger here; see my hands. Reach out your hand and put it into my side. Stop **doubting** and believe." (John 20:27) "But the man who has **doubts** is condemned if he eats, because his eating is not from faith; and everything that does not come from faith is sin." (Romans 14:23) "But when he asks, he must believe and not doubt, because he who **doubts** is like a wave of the sea, blown and tossed by the wind." (James 1:6)

Evil desires – "Therefore do not let sin reign in your mortal body so that you obey its **evil desires**." (Romans 6:12) "Put to death, therefore, whatever belongs to your earthly nature: sexual immorality, impurity, lust, **evil desires**, and greed, which is idolatry." (Colossians 3:5) "As obedient children, do not conform to the **evil desires** you had when you lived in ignorance." (1 Peter 1:14)

False doctrine – "...Stay there in Ephesus so that you may command certain men not to teach **false doctrines** any longer...." (I Timothy 1:3) "If anyone teaches **false doctrines** and does not agree to the sound instruction of our Lord Jesus Christ and to godly teaching he is conceited and understands nothing...." (I Timothy 6:3)

False prophets – "Watch out for **false prophets**. They come to you in sheep's clothing, but inwardly they are ferocious wolves." (Matthew 7:15) "At that time many will turn away from the faith and will betray and hate each other, and many **false prophets** will appear and deceive many people." (Matthew 24:10-11) "For false Christs and **false prophets** will appear and perform great signs and miracles to deceive even the elect—if that were possible." (Matthew 24:24) "Dear friends, do not believe every spirit, but test the spirits to see whether they are from God, because many **false prophets** have gone out into the world." (I John 4:1)

False teachers – "For the time will come when men will not put up with sound doctrine. Instead, to suit their own desires, they will gather around them a great number of **teachers** to say what their itching ears want to hear." (II Timothy 4:3) "But there were also false prophets among the people, just as there will be **false teachers** among you. Many will follow their shameful ways and will bring the way of truth into disrepute. In their greed these **teachers** will exploit you with stories they have made up. Their condemnation has long been hanging over them, and their destruction has not been sleeping." (II Peter 2:1-3)

Foolishness – "For the message of the cross is **foolishness** to those who are perishing, but to us who are being saved it is the power of God." (I Corinthians 1:18) "Jews demand miraculous signs and Greeks look for wisdom, but we preach Christ crucified: a stumbling block to Jews and

foolishness to Gentiles…." (I Corinthians 1:22-23) "The man without the Spirit does not accept the things that come from the Spirit of God, for they are **foolishness** to him, and he cannot understand them, because they are spiritually discerned." (I Corinthians 2:14)

Goats – "All the nations will be gathered before Him, and He will separate the people one from another as a shepherd separates the sheep from the **goats**. He will put the sheep on His right and the **goats** on His left." (Matthew 25:32-33) " (Hebrews 10:4)

Hardened hearts – "Then He climbed into the boat with them, and the wind died down. They were completely amazed, for they had not understood about the loaves; their **hearts** were **hardened**." (Mark 6:51-52) "Aware of their discussion, Jesus asked them: 'Why are you talking about having no bread? Do you still not see or understand? Are your **hearts hardened**?" (Mark 8:17) "He has blinded their eyes and **hardened** their **hearts**, so they can neither see with their eyes, nor understand with their **hearts**, nor turn—and I would heal them." (John 12:40)

Idolatry – "Do not be **idolaters**, as some of them were; as it is written: 'The people sat down to eat and drink and got up to indulge in pagan revelry." (I Corinthians 10:7) "Put to death, therefore, whatever belongs to your earthly nature: sexual immorality, impurity, lust, evil desires, and greed, which is **idolatry**." (Colossians 3:5) "For you have spent enough time in the past doing what pagans choose to do—living in debauchery, lust, drunkenness, orgies, carousing and detestable **idolatry**." (I Peter 4:3)

Idol worship – "You have lifted up the shrine of Molech and the star of your god Rphan, the idols you made to worship….." (Acts 7:43) "The rest of mankind that were not killed by these plagues still did not repent of the work of their hands; they did not stop **worshiping** demons and **idols** of gold, silver, bronze, stone and wood—idols that cannot see or hear or walk." (Revelation 9:20)

Ignorance – "In the past God overlooked such **ignorance**, but now He commands all people everywhere to repent." (Acts 17:30) "They are darkened in their understanding and separated from the life of God because of the **ignorance** that is in them due to the hardening of their hearts." (Ephesians 4:18)

Ignoring – "If anybody thinks he is a prophet or spiritually gifted, let him acknowledge that what I am writing to you is the Lord's command. If he **ignores** this, he himself will be **ignored**." (I Corinthians 14:37-38) "…How shall we escape if we **ignore** such a great salvation? This salvation, which was first announced by the Lord, was confirmed to us by those who heard Him." (Hebrews 2:3)

Liars – "We also know that law is made…for lawbreakers and rebels, the ungodly and sinful, the unholy and irreligious; for those who kill their fathers or mothers, for murderers, for adulterers and perverts, for slave traders and **liars** and perjurers…." (I Timothy 1:9-10) "The Spirit clearly says that in later times some will abandon the faith and follow deceiving spirits and things taught by demons. Such teachings come through hypocritical **liars**, whose consciences have been seared as with a hot iron." (I Timothy 4:1-2)

Neglect – "Woe to you, teachers of the law and Pharisees, you hypocrites! You give a tenth of your spices—mint, dill and cumin. But you have **neglected** the more important matters of the law—justice, mercy and faithfulness. You should have practiced the latter, without **neglecting** the former." (Matthew 23:23)

Obstinacy – "But some of them became obstinate; they refused to believe and publicly malign the Way." (Acts 19:9) "But concerning Israel He says, 'All day long I have held out My hands to a disobedient and **obstinate** people." (Romans 10:21)

Refusal – "These are the Scriptures that testify about me, yet you **refuse** to come to me to have life." (John 5:40) "Paul entered the synagogue and spoke boldly there for three months, arguing persuasively about the kingdom of God. But some of them became obstinate; they **refused** to believe…." (Acts 19:9) "….They perished because they **refused** to love the truth and so be saved." (II Thessalonians 2:10) "See to it that you do not **refuse** him who speaks. If they did not escape when they **refused** him who warned them on earth, how much less will we, if we turn away from Him who warns us from heaven." (Hebrews 12:25) "The fourth angel poured out his bowl on the sun, and the sun was given power to scorch people with fire. They were seared by the intense heat and they cursed the name of God, who had control over these plagues, but they **refused** to repent and glorify Him." (Revelation 16:8-9)

Rejection "He who listens to you listens to Me; he who **rejects** you **rejects** Me; but he who **rejects** Me **rejects** Him who sent Me." (Luke 10:16) "Whoever believes in the Son has eternal life, but whoever **rejects** the Son will not see life, for God's wrath remains on him." (John 3:36)"But for those who are self-seeking and who **reject** the truth and follow evil, there will be wrath and anger." (Romans 2:8) "Therefore, he who **rejects** this instruction does not **reject** man but God, who gives you His Holy Spirit." (I Thessalonians 4:8) "…I give you this instruction in keeping with the prophecies once made about you, so that by following them you may fight the good fight, holding on to faith and good conscience. Some have **rejected** these and so have shipwrecked their faith." (I Timothy 1:19)

Sin – "And if your right hand causes you to **sin**, cut it off and throw it away. It is better for you to lose one part of your body than for your whole body to go into hell." (Matthew 5:30) "Therefore, just as **sin** entered the world through one man, and death through **sin**, and in this way death came to all men, because all **sinned**—for before the law was given, **sin** was in the world. But **sin** is not taken into account when there is no law. Nevertheless, death reigned from the time of Adam to the time of Moses, even over those who did not **sin** by breaking a command, as Adam, who was a pattern of the one to come." (Romans 5:12-14) "For the wages of **sin** is death…." (Romans 6:23)

Sinners – "We know that God does not listen to **sinners**. He listens to the godly man who does His will." (John 9:31) "…See, the Lord is coming with thousands upon thousands of His holy ones to judge everyone, and to convict all the ungodly of all the ungodly acts they have done in the ungodly way, and of all the harsh words ungodly **sinners** have spoken against Him." (Jude 15)

Unbelief – " (Mark 16:16) "See to it, brothers, that none of you has a sinful, **unbelieving** heart that turns away from the living God." (Hebrews 3:12) "Anyone who believes in the Son of God has this testimony in his heart. Anyone who does **not believe** God has made Him out to be a liar, be he has **not believed** the testimony God has given about His Son." (I John 5:10) "But the cowardly, the **unbelieving**, the vile, the murderers, the sexually immoral, those who practice magic arts, the idolaters and all liars—their place will be in the fiery lake of burning sulfur. This is the second death." (Revelation 21:8)

Unforgiveness – "But if you do **not forgive** men the sins, your Father will **not forgive** your sins." (Matthew 6:15) "If you **forgive** anyone his sins, they are **forgiven**; if you do **not forgive** them, they are **not forgiven**." (John 20:23)

Unrepentant – "For John came to you to show you the way of righteousness, and you did not believe him, but the tax collectors and the prostitutes did. And even after you saw the, you did **not repent** and believe him." (Matthew 21:32) "But because of your stubbornness and your **unrepentant** heart, you are storing up wrath against yourself for the day of God's wrath when His righteous judgment will be revealed. God will give to each person according to what he has done." (Romans 2:5-6) "The rest of mankind that were not killed by these plagues sill did **not repent** of the work of their hands; they did not stop worshiping demons, and idols of bold, silver, bronze, stone and wood—idols that cannot see or hear or walk. Nor did they **repent** of their murders, their magic arts, their sexual immorality or their thefts." (Revelation 9:20)

HUMAN DESIRES

For further study: Romans and I Corinthians

Those who do not know the love of Christ have no spiritual guidance in their lives, so they are guided by their own desires for self-gratification. The wrongs that they do seem right because their consciences have never been awakened by the Spirit. There is some sense of good and evil in their lives, but with no spirituality in their lives, they either remain the same or grow spiritually worse. In Vacation Bible School, we had an example of salvation that was presented as either being on Man's By-way or on the King's Highway. The comparison was depicted as two parallel roads. Every human being is born into sin without any real knowledge of God. At any point in life, each person has the opportunity to move from Man's Highway onto the King's Highway, but God only gave one way to do this: The "Cross" road. Paul warns, "Brothers, we do not want you to be ignorant about those who fall asleep, or to grieve like the rest of men, who have no hope." (I Thessalonians 4:13) Those whose hope is not in the Lord really have nothing to hope for in life or death.

Arrogance – "...He (God) gave them over to a depraved mind, to do what ought not to be done. They have become filled with every kind of wickedness, evil, greed and depravity. They are full of envy, murder, strife deceit and malice. They are gossips, slanderers, God-haters insolent, **arrogant** and boastful...." (Romans 1:30) "This is especially true of those who follow the corrupt desire of the sinful nature and despise authority. Bold and **arrogant**, these men are not afraid to slander celestial beings...." (II Peter 2:10)

Boasting – "He chose the lowly things of this world and the despised things—and the things that are, so that no one may **boast** before Him." (I Corinthians 1:29) "For it is by grace you have been saved, through faith—and this not from yourselves. It is the gift of God—not by works, so that no one can **boast**. (Ephesians 2:8-9) "But if you harbor bitter envy and selfish ambition in your hearts, do not **boast** about it or deny the truth." (James 3:14) "As it is, you **boast** and brag. All such **boasting** is evil." (James 4:16) "These men are grumblers and faultfinders; they follow their own evil desires; they **boast** about themselves and flatter others for their own advantage." (Jude 1:16)

Busybodies – "We hear that some among you are idle. They are not busy; they are **busybodies**." (II Thessalonians 3:11) "…They get into the habit of being idle and going about from house to house. And not only do they become idlers, but also gossips and **busybodies**, saying things they ought not to." (I Timothy 5:13)

Carousing – "For you have spent enough time in the past doing what pagans choose to do—living in debauchery, lust, drunkenness, orgies, **carousing** and detestable idolatry." (I Peter 4:3)

Cravings – "For everything in the world—the **cravings** of sinful man, the lust of his eyes and the boasting of what he has and does—comes not from the Father but from the world." (I John 2:16)

Debauchery – "Let us behave decently, as in the daytime, not in orgies and drunkenness, not in sexual immorality and **debauchery**, not in dissension and jealousy." (Romans 13:13) "The acts of the sinful nature are obvious: sexual immorality, impurity and **debauchery**.…" (Galatians 5:19) "Do not get drunk on wine, which leads to **debauchery**.…" (Ephesians 5:18)

Dishonest gain – "Whoever can be trusted with very little can also be trusted with much, and whoever is **dishonest** with very little will also be **dishonest** with much." (Luke 16:10) "They must be silenced, because they are ruining whole households by teaching things they ought not to teach—and that for the sake of **dishonest gain**." (Titus 1:11)

Dissensions – "Let us behave decently…not in **dissension** and jealousy." (Romans 13:13)

Drunkenness – "Be careful, or your hearts will be weighed down with dissipation, **drunkenness** and the anxieties of life, and that day will close on you unexpectedly like a trap." (Luke 21:34) "Do not get **drunk** on wine…." (Ephesians 5:18) "For those who sleep, sleep at night, and those who get **drunk**, get **drunk** at night."(I Thessalonians 5:7)

Earthly nature (Earthly things) – "Their destiny is destruction, their god is their stomach, and their glory is in their shame. Their mind is on **earthly things**." (Philippians 3:19) "Put to death, therefore, whatever belongs to your **earthly nature**…." (Colossians 3:5) "But if you harbor bitter envy and selfish ambition in your hearts, do not boast about it or deny the truth. Such 'wisdom' does not come down from heaven but is **earthly**, unspiritual, of the devil." (James 3:14-15)

Evil desires – "They are the kind who worm their way into homes and gain control over weak-willed women, who are loaded down with sins and are swayed by all kinds of **evil desires**…." (II Timothy 3:6) "As obedient children, do not conform to the **evil desires** you had when you lived in ignorance." (I Peter 1:14) "First of all, you must understand that in the last days scoffers will come, scoffing and following their own **evil desires**." (II Peter 3:3)

Eyes – "But if your **eyes** are bad, your whole body will be full of darkness. If then the light within you is darkness, how great is that darkness!" (Matthew 6:23) "Why do you look at the speck of sawdust in your brother's **eye** and pay no attention to the plank in your own **eye**? How can you say to your brother, 'Let me take the speck out of your **eye**,' when all the time there is a plank in your own **eye**? You hypocrite, first take the plank out of your own **eye**, and then you will see clearly to remove the speck from your brother's **eye**." (Matthew 7:3-5) "He has blinded their **eyes** and deadened their hearts, so they can neither see with their **eyes**, nor understand with their hearts, nor turn—and I would heal them." (John 12:40)

Flattery – "For such people are not serving our Lord Christ, but their own appetites. By smooth talk and **flattery** they deceive the minds of naïve people." (Romans 16:18) "These men are grumblers and faultfinders; they follow their own evil desires; they boast about themselves and **flatter** others for their own advantage." (Jude 1:16)

Gratification – "…Do not think about how to **gratify** the desires of the sinful nature." (Romans 13:14) "So live by the spirit, and you will not

gratify the desires of the sinful nature." (Galatians 5:16) "All of us lived among them at one time, **gratifying** the cravings of our sinful thoughts. Like the rest, we were by nature objects of wrath." (Ephesians 2:3)

Greed – "Then He said to them, 'Watch out! Be on you guard against all kinds of **greed**; a man's life does not consist in the abundance of his possessions.' " (Luke 12:15) But among you there must not be even a hint of sexual immorality, or of any kind of impurity, or of **greed**, because these are improper for God's holy people…For of this you can be sure: No immoral, impure of **greedy** person—such a man is an idolater—has any inheritance in the kingdom of Christ and of God." (Ephesians 5:3-5)

Impurity – "Therefore God gave them over in the sinful desires of their hearts to sexual **impurity** for the degrading of their bodies with one another." (Romans 1:24) "The acts of the sinful nature are obvious: sexual immorality, **impurity** and debauchery…." (Galatians 5:19) "Having lost all sensitivity, they have given themselves over to sensuality so as to indulge in every kind of **impurity**, with a continual lust for more." (Ephesians 4:19)

Idleness – "And we urge you, brothers, warn those who are **idle**, encourage the timid, help the weak, be patient with everyone." (I Thessalonians 5:14) "In the name of our Lord Jesus Christ, we command you, brothers, to keep away from every brother who is **idle** and does not live according to the teaching you received from us….'If a man will not work, he shall not eat.' " (II Thessalonians 3:6-10)

Indecent acts – "In the same way the men also abandoned natural relations with women and were inflamed with lust for one another. Men committed **indecent acts** with other men, and received in themselves the due penalty for their perversion." (Romans 1:27)

Love of money – "For the **love of money** is a root of all kinds of evil. Some people, eager for **money**, have wandered from the faith and pierced themselves with many griefs." (I Timothy 6:10) "People will be lover of themselves, lovers of money, boastful, proud, abusive, disobedient to their parents…." (II Timothy 3:2)

Lovers of themselves – "But mark this: There will be terrible times in the last days. People will be **lovers of themselves**, lovers of money, boastful, proud, abusive, disobedient to the parents, ungrateful, unholy, without love, unforgiving, slanderous, without self-control brutal, not lovers of the good, treacherous, rash conceited, lovers of pleasure rather than lovers of God—having a form of godliness but denying its power. Have nothing to do with them." (II Timothy 3:1-5)

Lusts of the flesh – "The Spirit gives life; the **flesh** counts for nothing. The words I have spoken to you are spirit, and they are life…." (John 6:63)

Mockers – "Do not be deceived: God cannot be **mocked**. A man reaps what he sows." (Galatians 6:7)

Orgies – "Let us behave decently, as in the daytime, not in **orgies** and drunkenness, not in sexual immorality and debauchery, not in dissensions and jealousy." (Romans 13:13) "The acts of the sinful nature are obvious… envy, drunkenness, **orgies**, and the like." (Galatians 5:19-21)

Perversion – " 'O unbelieving and **perverse** generation,' Jesus replied, 'how long shall I stay with you? How long shall I put up with you?' " (Matthew 17:17) "You are a child of the devil and an enemy of everything that is right! You are full of all kinds of deceit and trickery. Will you never stop **perverting** the right ways of the Lord?" (Acts 13:10) "…Men committed indecent acts with other men, and received in themselves the due penalty for their **perversion**." (Romans 1:27) "

Riches – "It is easier for a camel to go through the eye of a needle than for a **rich** man to enter the kingdom of God" (Mark 10:25) "But woe to you who are **rich**, for you have already received you comfort." (Luke 6:24) "People who want to get **rich** fall into temptation and a trap and into many foolish and harmful desires that plunge men into ruin and destruction." (I Timothy 6:9) "They will say, 'The fruit you longed for is gone from you. All your **riches** and splendor have vanished, never to be recovered." (Revelation 18:14)

Scoffers – "Look, you **scoffers**, wonder and perish, for I am going to do something in your days that would never believe, even if someone told you.' " (Acts 13:41) "First of all, you must understand that in the last days **scoffers** will come, **scoffing** and following their own evil desires." (II Peter 3:3) "They said to you, 'In the last times there will be **scoffers** who will follow their own ungodly desires. These are the men who divide you, who follow mere natural instincts and do not have the Spirit.' " (Jude 1:18-19)

Selfish ambition – "Do nothing out of **selfish ambition** or vain conceit, but in humility consider others better than yourselves." (Philippians 2:3) "But if you harbor bitter envy and **selfish ambition** in your hearts, do not boast about it or deny the truth. Such 'wisdom' does not come down from heaven but is earthly, unspiritual, of the devil. For where you have envy and **selfish ambition**, there you find disorder and every evil practice." (James 3:14-16)

Self-indulgence – "Woe to you, teachers of the law and Pharisees, you hypocrites! You clean the outside of the cup and dish, but inside they are full of greed and **self-indulgence**." (Matthew 23:25) "You have lived on earth in luxury and **self-indulgence**. You have fattened yourselves in the day of slaughter." (James 5:5)

Sensuality – "Having lost all sensitivity, they have given themselves over to **sensuality** so as to indulge in every kind of impurity, with a continual lust for more." (Ephesians 4:19) "Such regulations indeed have an appearance of wisdom, with their self-imposed worship, their false humility and their harsh treatment of the body, but they lack any value in restraining **sensual** indulgence." (Colossians 2:23)

Sexual immorality – "For out of the heart come evil thoughts, murder, adultery, **sexual immorality**, theft, false testimony, slander." (Matthew 15:19) "…The body is not meant for **sexual immorality**, but for the Lord, and the Lord for the body." (I Corinthians 6:13) "Flee from **sexual immorality**. All other sins a man commits are outside his body, but he who sins **sexually** sins against his own body." Do you not know that your body is a temple of the Holy Spirit, who is in you, whom you have received from God? You are not your own; you were bought at a price. Therefore honor God with your body." (I Corinthians 6:18) "In a similar way, Sodom and Gomorrah and the surrounding towns gave themselves up to **sexual immorality** and perversion. They serve as an example of those who suffer the punishment of eternal fire." (Jude 1:7)

Sinful desires (Sinful nature) – "Although they claimed to be wise, they became fools and exchanged the glory of the immortal God for images made to look like mortal man and birds and animals and reptiles. Therefore God gave them over in the **sinful desires** of their hearts to sexual impurity for the degrading of their bodies with one another." (Romans 1:22-24) "Those who live according to the **sinful nature** have their minds set on what that **nature desires**; but those who live in minds set on what the Spirit desires. The mind of **sinful** man is death, but the mind controlled by the Spirit is life and peace; the **sinful mind** is hostile to God It does not submit to God's law, nor can it do so. Those controlled by the **sinful nature** cannot please God." (Romans 8:5-8)

Swindlers – "But now I am writing you that you must not associate with anyone who calls himself a brother but is sexually immoral or greedy, an idolater or a slanderer, a drunkard or a **swindler**. With such a man do not even eat." (I Corinthians 5:11) "Do you not know that the wicked will not inherit the kingdom of God? Do not be deceived: Neither the sexually immoral nor…**swindlers** will inherit the kingdom of God." (I Corinthians 6:9-10)

Unspiritual – "Do not let anyone who delights in false humility and the worship of angels disqualify you for the prize. Such a person goes into great detail about what he has seen, and his **unspiritual** mind puffs him up with idle notions." (Colossians 2:18) "But if you harbor bitter envy and selfish ambition in your hearts, do not boast about it or deny the truth. Such 'wisdom' does not come down from heaven but is earthly, **unspiritual**, of the devil."

Ignorance

For further study: II Corinthians chapter 11, Revelation

There are many reasons as to why a person does not know the truth about God and the salvation He gives to us trough His Son Jesus Christ. But at the same time, the Bible says that we are without excuse. We are also told that the heaves themselves declare the glory of God. Paul was one of those who not only refused to believe, but he took it upon himself to harass, arrest, and persecute Christians until he was personally confronted on the Road to Damascus. That event changed the rest of his life. He was in darkness until he actually came into the light and knowledge of Jesus Christ. A friend of mine recently reminded by of a training testimony we heard regularly from a co-worker. He would often say, "Even if you are only off by one degree, the farther you go, the more off course you become. I think this happens to many people today. They get off onto some tangent: self-gratification, false religion, or simply the lack of knowledge of the truth. Many seem to believe that, if they believe something to be true, that makes it truth for themselves. As stated in the knowledge section of this handbook, knowledge is only knowledge only if it really is the truth. Paul warns, "Timothy, guard what has been entrusted to your care. Turn away from godless chatter and the opposing ideas of what is falsely called knowledge, which some have professed and in so doing have wandered from the faith." (I Timothy 6:20)

Blindness – "He replied, 'Every plant that my heavenly Father has not planted will be pulled up by the roots. Leave them; they are **blind** guides. If a **blind** man leads a **blind** man, both will fall into a pit.' " (Matthew 15:13-14) "He has **blinded** their eyes and deadened their hearts, they can neither see with their eyes, nor understand with their hearts, nor turn—and I would heal them." (John 12:40) "But whoever hates his brother is in the darkness and walks around in the darkness; he does not know where he is going, because the darkness has **blinded** him." (I John 2:11)

Confusion – "The assembly was in **confusion:** Some were shouting one thing, some another. Most of the people did not even know why they were there." (Acts 19:32) "…Evidently some people are throwing you into **confusion** and are trying to pervert the gospel of Christ." (Galatians 1:7) "…The one who is throwing you into **confusion** will pay the penalty, whoever he may be." (Galatians 5:10)

Created things – "They exchanged the truth of God for a lie, and worshiped and served **created things** rather than the Creator—who is forever praised. Amen." (Romans 1:25)

Deception – "For such people are not serving our Lord Christ, but their own appetites. By smooth talk and flattery they **deceive** the minds of naïve people." (Romans 16:18) "But I am afraid that just as Eve was **deceived** by the serpent's cunning, your minds may somehow be led astray from your sincere and pure devotion to Christ." (II Corinthians 11:3) "Let no one **deceive** you with empty words, for because of such things God's wrath comes on those who are disobedient." (Ephesians 5:6)

Delusions – "They perish because they refused to love the truth and so be saved. For this reason God sends them a powerful **delusion** so that they will believe the lie and so that all will be condemned who have not believed the truth but have delighted in wickedness." (II Thessalonians 2:11) "But the beast was captured, and with him the false prophet who had performed the miraculous signs on his behalf. With these signs he had **deluded** those who had received the mark of the beast and worshiped his image. The two of them were thrown alive into the fiery lake of burning sulfur." (Revelation 19:20)

Doubts – "Immediately Jesus reached out His hand and caught him. 'You of little faith,' he said, 'why did you **doubt?**" (Matthew 14:31) "But when he asks, he must believe and not **doubt,** because he who **doubts** is like a wave of the sea, blown and tossed by the wind. That man should not think he will receive anything from the Lord; he is a double-minded man, unstable in all he does." (James 1:6-8)

Evil desires – "As obedient children, do not conform to the **evil desires** you had when you lived in ignorance." (I Peter 1:14) "Through these He has given us His very great and precious promises, so that through them you may participate in the divine nature and escape the corruption in the world caused by **evil desires**." (II Peter 1:4)

False apostles – "For such men are **false apostles**, deceitful workmen, masquerading as **apostles** of Christ. And no wonder, for Satan himself masquerades as an angel of light. It is not surprising, then, if his servants masquerade as servants of righteousness. Their end will be what their actions deserve." (II Corinthians 11:13) "I know your hard work and your perseverance. I know that you cannot tolerate wicked men, that you have tested those who claim to be **apostle** but are nor, and have found them **false**." (Revelation 2:2)

False brothers – "I have been constantly on the move. I have been in danger…from false brothers." (II Corinthians 11:26) "This matter arose because some false brothers had infiltrated our ranks to spy on the freedom we have in Christ Jesus and to make us slaves." (Galatians 2:4)

False Christs – "For **false Christs** and false prophets will appear and perform great signs and miracles to deceive even the elect—if that were possible." (Matthew 24:24) "For **false Christs** and false prophets will appear and perform signs and miracles to deceive the elect—if that were possible. So be on your guard; I have told you everything ahead of time." (Mark 13:22)

False doctrine – "As I urged you when I went into Macedonia, stay there in Ephesus so that you may command certain men not to teach **false doctrines** any longer nor to devote themselves to myths and endless genealogies. These promote controversies rather than God's work—which is by faith." (I Timothy 1:3-4) "If anyone teaches **false doctrines** and does not agree to the sound instruction of our Lord Jesus Christ and to godly teaching, he is conceited and understands nothing. He has an unhealthy interest in controversies and quarrels about words that result in envy, strife, malicious talk, evil suspicions and constant friction between men of corrupt mind…." (I Timothy 6:3-5)

False images (Graven images/idols) – "Do not make idols or set up an **image** or a sacred stone for yourselves, and do not place a carved stone in your land to bow down before it. I am the Lord your God." (Leviticus

26:1) "Cursed is the man who carves an **image** or casts an **idol**—a thing detestable to the Lord, the work of the craftsman's hands—and set it up in secret. Then all the people shall say, 'Amen.' " (Deuteronomy 27:15) "Although they claimed to be wise, they became fools and exchanged the glory of the immortal God for **images** made to look like mortal man and birds and animals and reptiles." (Romans 1:22-23)

False prophets – "Watch out for **false prophets**. They come to you in sheep's clothing, but inwardly they are ferocious wolves. By their fruit you will recognize them. Do people pick grapes from thorn bushes, or fits from thistles? Likewise every good tree bears good fruit, but a bad tree bears bad fruit." (Matthew 7:15) "...and many **false prophets** will appear and deceive many people." (Matthew 24:11) "Dear friends, do not believe every spirit, but test the spirits to see whether they are from God, because many **false prophets** have gone out into the world." (I John 4:1)

False testimony – "For out of the heart come evil thoughts, murder, adultery, sexual immorality, theft, **false testimony**, slander. These are what make a man 'unclean'; but eating with unwashed hands does not make him 'unclean.' " (Matthew 15:19) "...Do not murder, do not commit adultery, do not steal, do not give **false testimony**." (Matthew 19:19)

False witnesses – "The chief priests and the whole Sanhedrin were looking for false evidence against Jesus so that they could put Him to death. But they did not find any, though many **false witnesses** came forward." (Matthew 26:59-60) "They produced **false witnesses**, who testified, 'This fellow never stops speaking against this holy place and against the law.' " (Acts 6:13)

Falsehood – "Therefore each of you must put off **falsehood** and speak truthfully to his neighbor, for we are all members of one body." (Ephesians 4:25) "We are from God, and whoever knows God listens to us; but whoever is not from God does not listen to us. This is how we recognize the Spirit of truth and the spirit of **falsehood**." (I John 4:6) "Outside are the dogs, those who practice magic arts, the sexually immoral, the murderers, the idolaters, and everyone who loves and practices **falsehood**." (Revelation 22:15)

Heresy – "But there were also false prophets among the people, just as there will e false teachers among you. The will secretly introduce destructive

heresies, even denying the sovereign Lord who bought them—bringing swift destruction on themselves." (II Peter 2:1)

Lies – "You belong to your father, the devil, and you want to carry out your father's desire. He was a murderer from the beginning, not holding to the truth, tor there is no truth in him. When he **lies**, he speaks his native language, for he is a **liar** and the father of **lies**." (John 8:44) "Then Peter said, 'Ananias, how is it that Satan has so filled you heart that you have **lied** to the Holy Spirit and have kept for yourself some of the money you received for the land?' …When Ananias heard this, he fell down and died." (Acts 5:3-5) "They exchanged the truth of God for a **lie**, and worshiped and served created things rather than the Creator—who is forever praised. Amen." (Romans 1:25)

Magic arts – "They followed him because he had amazed them for a long time with his magic." (Acts 8:11) "Nor did they repent of their murders, their **magic arts**, their sexual immorality or their thefts." (Revelation 9:21) "But the cowardly, the unbelieving, the vile, the murderers, the sexually immoral, those who practice **magic arts**, the idolaters, and all liars—their place will be in the fiery lake of burning sulfur. This is the second death." (Revelation 21:8)

Not hearing – "Paul took the road through the interior and arrived at Ephesus. There he found some disciples and asked them, 'Did you receive the Holy Spirit when you believed?' They answered, 'No, we have **not** even **heard** that there is a Holy Spirit.'" (Acts 19:2) "How, then, can they call on the one they have not believed in? And how can they believe in the one of whom they have **not heard**? And how can they **hear** without someone preaching to them?" (Romans 10:14)

Reprobate minds (Corrupt/Depraved minds) – "And even as they did not like to retain God in their knowledge, God gave them over to a **reprobate** mind, to do those things which are not convenient.…" (Romans 1:28) (KJV) "He has an unhealthy interest in controversies and quarrels about words that result in envy, strife, malicious talk, evil suspicions and constant friction between men of **corrupt mind**, who have been robbed of the truth and who think that godliness is a means to financial gain." (I Timothy 6:4-5) "Just as Jannes and Jambres opposed Moses, so also these men oppose the truth—men of **depraved minds**, who, as far as the faith is concerned, are rejected. But they will not get very far because, as in the case of those men, their folly will be clear to everyone." (II Timothy 3:8-9)

Satan – "Some people are like seed along the path, where the word is sown. As soon as they hear it, **Satan** comes and takes away the word that was sown in them." (Mark 4:15) "…**Satan** himself masquerades as an angel of light." (II Corinthians 11:14) "The coming of the lawless one will be in accordance with the work of **Satan** displayed in all kinds of counterfeit miracles, signs, and wonders…." (II Thessalonians 2:9) "Some have in fact already turned away to follow **Satan**." (I Timothy 5:15)

Unrepentance – "Then Jesus began to denounce the cities in which most of His miracles had been performed, because they did **not repent**." (Matthew 11:20) "The rest of mankind that were not killed by these plagues still did **not repent** of the work of their hands; they did not stop worshiping demons, and idol of gold, silver, bronze, stone and wood…." (Revelation 9:20)

Walking in darkness – "Then Jesus told them, 'You are going to have the light just a little while longer. **Walk** while you have the light, before **darkness** overtakes you. The man who **walks in the dark** does not know where he is going.' " (John 12:35) "Anyone who claims to be in the light but hates his brother is still **in** the **darkness**. Whoever loves his brother lives in the light, and there is nothing in him to make him stumble. But whoever hates his brother is **in the darkness** and **walks** around **in the darkness**; he does not know where he is going, because the **darkness** has blinded him." (I John 1:9-11) (I John 2:11)

Wandering from faith – "Timothy, guard what has been entrusted to your care. Turn away from godless chatter and the opposing ideas of what is falsely called knowledge, which some have professed and in so doing have **wandered from the faith**." (I Timothy 6:20-21)

Worship of angels – "Do not let anyone who delights in false humility and the **worship of angels** disqualify you for the prize. Such a person goes into great detail about what he has seen, and his unspiritual mind puffs him up with idle notions." (Colossians 2:18)

Uncontrolled

For further study: Romans chapter 7; James chapter 3

Those who are saved through the blood sacrifice of Jesus Christ and have been filled with His Spirit are controlled by the Spirit in their daily lives. This is not to say that we have no sin because the Bible tells us, "If we claim to be without sin, we deceive ourselves and the truth is not in us." (I John 1:8)The difference is that we have been forgiven of our sins, but we still are human and susceptible to all the temptations that Satan puts before us. We have to continually submit ourselves to God through Jesus Christ in order to overcome these temptations. The following, I am sure, is only a partial list of the ways that we as human beings lack self-control in our lives and must turn to God to help us.

Anger – "In your **anger** do not sin. Do not let the sun go down while you are still **angry**, and do not give the devil a foothold." (Ephesians 4:26-28) "My dear brothers, take note of this: Everyone should be quick to listen, slow to speak, and slow to become **angry**, for man's **anger** does not bring about the righteous life that God desires." (James 1:19-20)

Bodily sin – "Therefore do not let **sin** reign in your mortal **body** so that you obey its evil desires. Do not offer the parts of your **body** to **sin**, as instruments of wickedness, but rather offer yourselves to God, as those who have been brought from death to life; and offer the parts of your **body** to Him as instruments of righteousness." (Romans 6:12-13) "For if you live according to the **sinful** nature, you will die; but if by the Spirit you put to death the misdeeds of the **body**, you will live." (Romans 8:13) "Flee from sexual immorality. All other **sins** a man commits are outside his **body**, but he who **sins** sexually **sins** against his own **body**." (I Corinthians 6:18)

Cursing – "For God said, 'Honor you father and mother' and 'Anyone who **curses** his father or mother must be put to death.' " (Matthew 15:4) "With the tongue we praise our Lord and Father, and with it we **curse** men, who have been made in God's likeness. Out of the same mouth come praise and **cursing**. My brothers, this should not be." (James 3:9)

Fear – "Then all the people of the region of the Gerasenes asked Jesus to leave them, because they were overcome with **fear**. So He got into the boat and left." (Luke 8:37) "But I will show you whom you should **fear**: **Fear** him who, after the killing of the body, has power to throw you into hell. Yes, I tell you, **fear** him." (Luke 12:5) "Everyone who does evil hates the light, and will not come into the light for **fear** that his deeds will be exposed." (John 3:20)

Hostility – "…the sinful mind is **hostile** to God. It does not submit to God's law, nor can it do so. Those controlled by the sinful nature cannot please God." (Romans 8:7) "…You suffered from you own countrymen the same things those churches suffered from the Jews, who killed the Lord Jesus and the prophets and also drove us out. The displease God and are **hostile** to all men…." (I Thessalonians 2:14-15)

Indulgence – "Such regulations indeed have an appearance of wisdom, with their self-imposed worship, their false humility and their harsh treatment of the body, but they lack any value in restraining sensual **indulgence**." (Colossians 2:23) "You have lived on earth in luxury and self-**indulgence**. You have fattened yourselves in the day of slaughter." (James 5:5)

Lack of self-control – "The wife's body does not belong to her alone but also to her husband. In the same way, the husband's body does not belong to him alone but also to his wife. Do not deprive each other except by mutual consent and for a time, so that you may devote yourselves to prayer. Then come together again so that Satan will not tempt you because of you **lack of self-control**." (I Corinthians 7:5)

Persecution of Saints – "They were stoned; they were sawed in two; they were put to death by the sword. They went about in sheepskins and goatskins, destitute, **persecuted** and mistreated—the world was not worthy of them. They wandered in deserts and mountains, and in caves and holes in the ground." (Hebrews 11:37)

Poisoned minds – "But the Jews who refused to believe stirred up the Gentiles and **poisoned** their **minds** against the brothers." (Acts 14:2)

Quarreling – "You are still worldly. For since there is jealousy and **quarreling** among you, are you not worldly? Are you not acting like mere men?" (I Corinthians 3:3) "Don't have anything to do with foolish and stupid arguments, because you know they produce **quarrels**." (II Timothy 2:23) "What causes fights and quarrels among you? Don't they come from your desires that battle within you? You want something but don't get it. You kill and covet, but you cannot have what you want. You **quarrel** and fight. You do not have, because you do not ask God." (James 4:1-2)

Sinful nature (Sinful passions) – "For when we were controlled by the **sinful nature**, the **sinful passions** aroused by the law were at work in our bodies, so that we bore fruit for death." (Romans 7:5) "Those controlled by the **sinful nature** cannot please God." (Romans 8:8) "For the **sinful nature** desires what is contrary to the Spirit, and the Spirit what is contrary to the **sinful nature**. They are in conflict with each other, so that you do not do what you want." (Galatians 5:17-19)

Slander – "Why not say—as we are being **slanderously** reported as saying and as some claim that we say—'Let us do evil that good may result'? Their condemnation is deserved." (Romans 3:8) "So I counsel younger widows to marry, to have children, to manage their homes and to give the enemy no opportunity for **slander**." (I Timothy 5:14) "Likewise, teach older women to be reverent in the way they live, not to be **slanderers** or addicted to much wine, but to teach what is good." (Titus 2:3)

Slaves to sin – "Jesus replied, 'I tell you the truth, everyone who sins is a **slave to sin**. Now a **slave** has no permanent place in the family, but a son belongs to it forever.' " (John 8:34) "Don't you know that when you offer yourselves to someone to obey him as **slaves**, you are **slaves** to the one whom you obey—whether you are **slaves to sin**, which leads to death, or to obedience, which leads to righteousness? But thanks be to God that, though you used to be **slaves to sin**, you whole-heartedly obeyed the form of teaching to which you were entrusted. You have been set free from **sin** and have become **slaves** to righteousness." (Romans 6:16-18)

Stealing – "He who has been **stealing** must **steal** no longer, but must work, doing something useful with his own hands, that he may have something to share with those in need." (Ephesians 4:28)

Tongue – "Their throats are open graves; their **tongues** practice deceit. The poison of vipers is on their lips. Their mouths are full of cursing and bitterness." (Romans 3:13) If anyone considers himself religious and yet does not keep a tight rein on his **tongue**, he deceives himself and his religion is worthless. Religion that God our Father accepts as pure and faultless is this: to look after the orphans and widows in their distress and to keep oneself from being polluted by the world." (James 1:26) "Likewise the **tongue** is a small part of the body, but it makes great boasts. Consider what a great forest is set on fire by a small spark. The **tongue** also is a fire, a world of evil among the parts of the body. It corrupts the whole person, set the whole course of his life on fire, and is itself set on fire by hell." (James 3:5-6)

Temptations – "And lead us not into **temptation**, but deliver us from the evil one." (Matthew 6:13) "No **temptation** has seized you except what is common to man. And God is faithful; He will not let you be **tempted** beyond what you can bear. But when you are **tempted**, He will also provide a way out so that you can stand up under it." (I Corinthians 10:13) "When **tempted**, no one should say, 'God is **tempting** me.' For God cannot be **tempted** by evil, nor does He **tempt** anyone, but each one is **tempted** when, by his own evil desire, he is dragged away and enticed. Then, after desire has conceived, it gives birth to sin; and sin, when it is full-grown, gives birth to death." (James 1:13-15)

Unforgiving – "For if you **forgive** men when they sin against you, your heavenly Father will also **forgive** you, but if you do **not forgive** men their sins, your Father will **not forgive** your sins." (Matthew 6:14-15) "**Forgive** us our sins, for we also **forgive** everyone who sins against us." (Luke 11:4)

Weakness – "Watch and pray so that you will not fall into temptation. The spirit is willing, but the body is **weak**." (Matthew 26:41) "Be careful that the exercise of your freedom does not become a stumbling block to the **weak**. For if anyone with a **weak** conscience sees you who have this knowledge eating in an idol's temple, won't he be emboldened to eat what has been sacrificed to idols? So this **weak** brother, for whom Christ died, is destroyed by your knowledge. When you sin against your brothers in this way and wound their **weak** conscience, you sin against Christ. Therefore, if what I eat causes by brother to fall into sin, I will never eat meat again, so that I will not cause him to fall." (I Corinthians 8:9-12)

Wild living – "Not long after that, the younger son got together all he had, set off for a distant country and there squandered his wealth in **wild living**." (Luke 15:13) "They are **wild** waves of the sea, foaming up their shame; wandering stars, for whom blackest darkness has been reserved forever." (Jude 1:13)

Worldly passions – "For the grace of God that brings salvation has appeared to all men. It teaches us to say 'No' to ungodliness and **worldly passions**, and to live self-controlled, upright and godly lives in this present age." (Titus 2:12)

Impatience

For Further Study: Deuteronomy chapter 28, Book of Job

Proverbs 19:11 tells us, "A man's wisdom gives him patience; it is to his glory to overlook an offense." (Proverbs 19:11) Job is the Biblical example of a man with patience. God allowed Satan to test Job to see if he would deny God, but despite all of his losses, Job refused to do so. His friends tried to dissuade his from his determined course, but Job persisted and was rewarded for his constancy.

James compares a man's patience to that of a farmer awaiting the harvest of his crops: "Be patient then, brothers, until the Lord's coming, See how the farmer waits for the land to yield its valuable crop and how patient he is for the autumn and spring rains." He goes on to say, "You too, be patient and stand fir, because the Lord's coming is near. Don't grumble against each other, brothers, or you will be judged. The Judge is standing at the door!" (James 5:7-9) The word "impatient" is only used three times in the New International Version of the Bible, but its concepts are dealt with throughout.

Affliction – "If you remain hostile toward me and refuse to listen to me, I will multiply your **afflictions** seven times over, as you sins deserve." (Leviticus 26:21) "The Lord will **afflict** you with the boils of Egypt and with tumors, festering sores and the itch, from which you cannot be cures. The Lord will **afflict** you with madness, blindness and confusion of the mind." (Deuteronomy 28:27-28)

Anger – "In your **anger** do not sin…." (Psalm 4:4) "Refrain from **anger** and turn from wrath." (Psalm 37:8) "A gentle answer turns away wrath, but a harsh word stirs up **anger**." (Proverbs 15:1) "A fool gives full vent to his **anger**, but a wise man keeps himself under control." (Proverbs 29:11) "A man's **anger** does not bring about the righteous life that God desires." (James 1:20)

Anguish – "My life is consumed by **anguish** and my years by groaning; my strength fails because of my affliction." (Psalm 31:10) "I am feeble and utterly crushed; I groan in **anguish** of heart." (Psalm 38:8)

Anxiety – "Do not be **anxious** about anything, but in everything, by prayer and petition, with thanksgiving, present you requests to God." (Philippians 4:6) "So then, banish **anxiety** from you r heart and cast off the troubles of your body, for youth and vigor are meaningless." (Ecclesiastes 11:10) "Cast all your **anxiety** upon Him because He cares for you." (I Peter 5:7)

Burdens – "For my yoke is easy and my **burden** is light." (Matthew 11:30) "Obey your leaders and submit to their authority. They keep watch over you as men who must give an account. Obey them so that their work will be a joy, nor a **burden**, for that would be of no advantage to you." (Hebrews 13:17)

Complaining – "Why should any living man **complain** when punished for his sins?" (Lamentations 3:39) "How long will this wicked community grumble against me? I have heard the **complaints** of these grumbling Israelites." (Numbers 14:27) "Do everything without **complaining** or arguing." (Philippians 2:14)

Contempt- "Let their lying lips be silenced, for with pride and **contempt** they speak arrogance against the righteous." (Psalm 31:18) "He who obeys instruction guards his life, but he who is **contemptuous** of His ways will die." (Proverbs 16:19) "Or do you show **contempt** for the riches of His kindness, tolerance, and patience, not realizing that God's kindness leads you toward repentance?" (Romans 2:4)

Criticism – "We want to avoid any **criticism** of the way we administer this liberal gift." (II Corinthians 8:20)

Envy – "Resentment kills a fool, and **envy** slays the simple." (Job 5:2) "Let us not become conceited, provoking and **envying** each other."(Galatians 5:26) "For where you have **envy** and selfish ambition, there you find disorder and every evil practice." (James 3:16)

Hostility – "…The sinful mind is **hostile** to God. It does not submit to God's law, nor can it do so. Those controlled by the sinful nature cannot please God." (Romans 8:7) "They displease God and are **hostile** to all men in their effort to keep us from speaking to the Gentiles so that they may be saved. In this way they always heap up their sins to the limit. The wrath of God has come upon them at last." (I Thessalonians 2:15-16)

Jealousy – "Anger is cruel and fury overwhelming, but who can stand before **jealousy**?" (Proverbs 27:4) "The Lord is a **jealous** and avenging God; the Lord takes vengeance and is filled with wrath. The lord takes vengeance on His foes and maintains His wrath against His enemies." (Nahum 1:2) "Neither their silver nor their gold will be able to save them on the day of the Lord's wrath. In the fire of His **jealousy** the whole world will be consumed, for He will make a sudden end of all who live on earth." (Zephaniah 1:18) "You are still worldly. For since there is **jealousy** and quarreling among you, are you not worldly? Are you not acting like mere men?" (I Corinthians 3:3)

Judging – "You therefore, have no excuse, you who pass **judgment** on someone else, for at whatever point you **judge** the other, you are condemning yourself, because you who pass **judgment** do the same things. Now we know that God's **judgment** against those who do such things is based on truth. So when you, a mere man, pass **judgment** on them and yet do the same things, do you think you will escape God's **judgment**?" (Romans 2:1-3)

Persecution – "The one who received the seed that fell on rocky places is the man who hears the word and at once receives it with joy. But since he has no root, he lasts only a short time. When trouble or **persecution** comes because of the word, he quickly falls away." (Matthew 13:20-21) "Who shall separate us from the love of Christ? Shall trouble or hardship or **persecution** or famine or nakedness or danger or sword?" (Romans 8:35) "Do not be afraid of what you are about to suffer. I tell you, the devil will put some of you in prison to test you, and you will suffer **persecution** for ten days. Be faithful, even to the point of death, and I will give the crown of life." (Revelation 2:10)

Poisonous lips (tongue) – "They make their **tongues** as sharp as a serpent's; the **poison** of vipers is on their **lips**." (Psalm 140:3) "…but no man can tame the **tongue**. It is a restless evil, full of deadly **poison**." (James 3:8)

Rage – "A man's own folly ruins his life, yet his heart **rages** against the Lord." (Proverbs 19:3) "All who **rage** against you will surely be ashamed and disgraced; those who oppose you will be as nothing and perish." (Isaiah 41:11)

Suffering – "For it is commendable if a man bears up under the pain of unjust **suffering** because he is conscious of God." (I Peter 2:19) "And the God of all grace, who called you to His eternal glory in Christ, after you have **suffered** for a little while, will Himself restore you and make you strong, firm and steadfast."(I Peter 5:10)

Temper – "A patient man has great understanding, but a quick-**tempered** man displays folly." (Proverbs 14:29) "A hot-**tempered** man stirs up dissension, but a patient man calms a quarrel." (Proverbs 15:18)

Trouble – "The Lord is a refuge for the oppressed, a stronghold in the times of trouble." (Psalm 9:9) "The righteous cry out, and the Lord hears them; he delivers them from all their **troubles**." (Psalm 34:17) "Therefore do not worry about tomorrow, for tomorrow will worry about itself. Each day has enough **trouble** of its own." (Matthew 6:34) "There will be **trouble** and distress for every man who does evil: first for the Jew and then for the Gentile…." (Romans 2:9)

Weariness – "Come to me all you who are weary and burdened, and I will give you rest." (Matthew 11:28) "Let us not become **weary** in doing good, for at the proper time we will reap a harvest if we do not give up." (Galatians 6:9)

Worry – "Therefore I tell you, do not **worry** about your life, what you will eat or drink; or about your body, what you will wear. Is not life for important than food, and the body more important than clothes? Look at the birds of the air; they do not sow or reap or store away in barns, and yet you heavenly Father feeds them. Are you not much more valuable than they? Who of you by **worrying** can add a single hour to his life? And why do you worry about clothes? See how the lilies of the field grow. They do not labor or spin. Yet I tell you that not even Solomon in all his splendor was dressed like one of these. If that is how God clothes the grass of the field, which is here today and tomorrow is thrown into the fire, will He not much more clothe you, O you of little faith? So do not **worry**, saying, 'What shall we eat?' or 'What shall we drink?' or 'What shall we wear?' For the pagans run after all these things, and your heavenly Father knows that you need them. But seek first

His kingdom and His righteousness, and all these things will be given to you as well. Therefore do not **worry** about tomorrow, for tomorrow will **worry** about itself. Each day has enough trouble of its own." (Matthew 6:25-34)

Ungodliness

For further study: the books of Proverbs and Matthew

This topic will include ungodly beings, ungodly behavior, and the warnings and pending punishments for such. God has an expectation of all His creatures to be like Him, but we rebel and seek our own worldly pleasures. The Bible uses the word "pagans" to describe the people who neither love nor seek to please God. Paul describes the last days as follows: "But mark this: There will be terrible times in the last days. People will be lovers of themselves, lovers of money, boastful, proud, abusive, disobedient to their parents, ungrateful, unholy, without love, unforgiving, slanderous, without self-control, brutal, not lovers of the good, treacherous, rash, conceited, lovers of pleasure rather than lovers of God—having a form of godliness but denying its power. Have nothing to do with them." (II Timothy 3:1-5) If these words, written two thousand years ago, do not describe today's world, I don't know what does!

Abandoning God (Faith) – "The Spirit clearly say that in later times some will **abandon the faith** and follow deceiving spirits and things taught by demons. Such teachings come through hypocritical liars, whose consciences have been seared as with a hot iron. They forbid people to marry and order them to abstain from certain foods which God created to be received with thanksgiving by those who believe and who know the truth. For everything God created is good, and nothing is to be rejected if it is received with thanksgiving, because it is consecrated by the word of God and prayer." (I Timothy 4:1-5)

Angel of light (Satan) – "For such men are false apostles, deceitful workmen, masquerading as apostles of Christ and no wonder, for Satan himself masquerades as an **angel of light**. It is not surprising, then, if his servants masquerade as servants or righteousness. Their end will be what their actions deserve." (II Corinthians 11:13-14)

Beelzebub – "...If the head of the house has been called **Beelzebub**, how much more the members of his household!" (Matthew 10:25) "Jesus knew their thoughts and said to them: 'Any kingdom divided against itself will be ruined, and a house divided against itself will fall. If Satan is divided against himself, how can his kingdom stand? I say this because you claim that I drive out demons by **Beelzebub**. Now if I drive out demons by **Beelzebub**, by whom do your followers drive them out? So then, they will be your judges. But if I drive out demons by the finger of God, then the kingdom of God has come to you.' " (Luke 11: 17-20)

Blasphemy – "He who is not with me is against me, and he who does not gather with me scatters. And so I tell you, every sin and **blasphemy** will be forgiven men, but the **blasphemy** against the Spirit will not be forgiven. Anyone who speaks a word against the Son of Man will be forgiven, but anyone who speaks against the Holy Spirit will not be forgiven, either in this age or in the age to come." (Matthew 12:30-32) "...Bold and arrogant, these men are not afraid to slander celestial beings; yet even angels, although they are stronger and more powerful, do not bring slanderous accusations against such beings in the presence of the Lord. But these men **blaspheme** in matters they do not understand. They are like brute beasts, creatures of instinct, born only to be caught and destroyed, and like beasts they too will perish." (II Peter 2:10-12)

Condemnation – "He said unto them, 'Go into all the world and preach the good news to all creation. Whoever believes and is baptized will be saved, but whoever does not believe will be **condemned**.' " (Mark 16:15-16) "...all will be **condemned** who have not believed the truth but have delighted in wickedness." (II Thessalonians 2:12) "In their greed these teachers will with stories they have made up. Their **condemnation** has long been hanging over them, and their destruction has not been sleeping." (II Peter 2:3)

Darkness – "But the subjects of the kingdom will be thrown outside, into the darkness, where there will be weeping and gnashing of teeth."

(Matthew 8:12) "Your eye is the lamp of your body. When your eyes are good, your whole body also is full of light. But when they are bad, your body also is full of **darkness**. See to it, then, that the light within you is not **darkness**. Therefore, if you whole body is full of light, and not part of it is **dark**, it will be completely lighted, as when the light of a lamp shines on you." (Luke 11:34-36) "The light shines in the **darkness**, but the **darkness** has not understood it." (John 1:5)

Debauchery – "I am afraid that when I come again my God will be grieved over many who have sinned earlier and have not repented of the impurity, sexual sin and **debauchery** in which they have indulged." (II Corinthians 12:21) "The acts of the sinful nature age obvious: sexual immorality, impurity and **debauchery**...." (Galatians 5:19) "For you have spent enough time in the past doing what pagans choose to do—living in **debauchery**, lust drunkenness, orgies, carousing and detestable idolatry." (I Peter 4:3)

Demons – "Do I mean then that a sacrifice offered to an idol is anything, or that an idol is anything? No, but the sacrifices of pagans are offered to **demons**, not to God, and I do not want you to be participants with **demons**. You cannot drink the cup of the Lord and the cup of **demons** too; you cannot have a part in both the Lord 's Table and the table of **demons**. Are we trying to arouse the Lord's jealousy? Are we stronger than He?" (I Corinthians 10:19-22) "The Spirit clearly says that in later times some will abandon the faith and follow deceiving spirits and thing taught by **demons**." (I Timothy 4:1) "They are spirits of **demons** performing miraculous signs, and they go out to the kings of the whole world, to gather them for the battle on the great day of God Almighty." (Revelation 16:14)

Denial – "They claim to know God, but by their actions they **deny** Him. They are detestable, disobedient and unfit for doing anything good." (Titus 1:16) "For certain men whose condemnation was written about long ago have secretly slipped in among you. They are godless men, who change the grace of out God into a license for immorality and **deny** Jesus Christ our only Sovereign and Lord." (Jude 1:4)

Detestable things – "There are six things the Lord hates, seven that are **detestable** to Him: haughty eyes, a lying tongue, hands that shed innocent blood, a heart that devises wicked schemes, feet that are quick to rush into evil, a false witness who pours out lies and a man who stirs up dissension among brothers." (Proverbs 6:16-19) "The Pharisees, who loved money, heard all this and were sneering at Jesus. He said to them, 'You are the ones who justify yourselves in the eyes of men, but God knows your hearts. What is highly valued among men is **detestable** in God's sight.' " (Luke 16:14-15)

Devil – "You belong to your father, the **devil**, and you want to carry out your father's desire. He was a murderer from the beginning, not holding to the truth, for there is not truth in him. When he lies, he speaks his native language, for he is a liar and the father of lies." (John 8:44) "Submit yourselves, then, to God. Resist the **devil**, and he will flee from you." (James 4:7) "He who does what is sinful is of the **devil**, because the **devil** has been sinning from the beginning. The reason the Son of God appeared was to destroy the **devil's** work." (I John 3:8) "The great dragon was hurled down—that ancient serpent called the **devil**, or Satan, who leads the whole world astray. He was hurled to the earth, and his angels with him." (Revelation 12:9)

Dishonesty – "Whoever can be trusted with very little can also be trusted with much, and whoever is **dishonest** with very little will also be **dishonest** with much." (Luke 16:10) "For there are many rebellious people, mere talkers and deceivers, especially those of the circumcision group. They must be silenced, because they are ruining whole households by teaching things they ought not to teach—and that for the sake of **dishonest** gain." (Titus 1:11)

Disobedience – "Just as you who were at one time **disobedient** to God have now received mercy as a result of their **disobedience**, so they too have now become **disobedient** in order that they too may now receive mercy as a result of God's mercy to you. For God has bound all men over to **disobedience** so that He may have mercy on them all." (Romans 11:30-32) "Let no one deceive you with empty words, for because of such things God's wrath comes on those who are **disobedient**." (Ephesians 5:6) "It still remains that some will enter that rest, and those who formerly had the gospel preached to them did not go in, because of their **disobedience**." (Hebrews 4:6)

Evil Spirits (Wicked Spirits) – "When an **evil spirit** comes out of a man, it goes through arid places seeking rest and does not find it. Then it says, 'I will return to the house I left. When it arrives, it finds the house unoccupied, swept clean and put in order. Then it goes and takes with it seven other **spirits** more **wicked** than itself, and they go in and live there. And the final condition of that man is worse than the first. That is how it will be with this **wicked** generation."(Matthew 12:43-45) "Calling the Twelve to Him, He sent them out two by two and gave them authority over **evil spirits**." (Mark 6:7)

Godless chatter – "Timothy, guard what has been entrusted to your care. Turn away from **godless chatter** and the opposing ideas of what is falsely called knowledge, which some have professed and in so doing have wandered from the faith. Grace be with you." (I Timothy 6:20-21) "Avoid **godless chatter**, because those who indulge in it will become more and more ungodly." (II Timothy 2:16)

Idol worship – "For all the gods of the nations are **idols**, but the Lord made the heavens." (Psalm 96:5) "You have lifted up the shrine of Molech and the star of your god Rephan, the **idols** you made to **worship** therefore I will send you into exile beyond Babylon." (Acts 7:43) "While Paul was waiting for them in Athens, he was greatly distressed to see that the city was full of **idols**." (Acts 17:16) "You know that when you were pagans, somehow or other you were influenced and led astray to mute **idols**." (I Corinthians 12:2) "Dear children, keep yourselves from **idols**." (I John 5:21)

Immorality – "Since there is so much **immorality**, each man should have his own wife, and each woman her own husband." (I Corinthians 7:2) "We should not commit sexual **immorality**, as some of them did—and in one day twenty-three thousand of them died." (I Corinthians 10:8)

Impurity – "Now your **impurity** is lewdness. Because I tried to cleanse you but you would not be cleansed from your **impurity**, you will not be clean again until my wrath against you has subsided."(Ezekiel 24:13) "Therefore God gave them over in the sinful desires of their hearts to sexual **impurity** for the degrading of their bodies with one another. They exchanged the truth of God for a lie, and worshiped and served created things rather than the Creator—who is forever praised. Amen. (Romans 1:24-25) (Galatians 5:19)

Insulting the spirit – "How much more severely do you think a man deserves to be punished who has trampled the Son of God underfoot, who has treated as an unholy thing the blood of the covenant that sanctified him, and who has **insulted the Spirit** of grace?" (Hebrews 10:29)

Irreligious – "We also know that law is made not for the righteous but for lawbreakers and rebels, the ungodly and sinful, the unholy and **irreligious**; for those who kill their fathers or mothers, for murderers, for adulterers and perverts, for slave traders and liars and perjurers—and for whatever else is contrary to the sound doctrine…." (I Timothy 1:9-10)

Lawbreakers – "The one who is not circumcised physically and yet obeys the **law** will condemn you who, even though you have the written code and circumcision, are a **lawbreaker**." (Romans 2:27) "But if you show favoritism, you sin and are convicted by the **law** as **lawbreakers**. For whoever keeps the whole **law** and yet stumbles at just one point is guilty of breaking all of it. For he who said, 'Do not commit adultery,' also said 'Do not murder.' If you do not commit adultery but do commit murder, you have become a **lawbreaker**." (James 2:9-11)

Lovers of themselves – "People will be **lovers of themselves**, lovers of money, boastful, proud, abusive, disobedient to their parents, ungrateful, unholy, without love, unforgiving, slanderous, without self-control, brutal, not lovers of the good…." (II Timothy 3:2)

Pagans – "And when you pray, do not keep on *babbling* like **pagans**, for they think they will be heard because of their many words. Do not be like them, for your Father knows what you need before you ask Him." (Matthew 6:7) "Live such good lives among the **pagans** that, though they accuse you of doing wrong, they may see your good deeds and glorify God on the day He visits us." (I Peter 2:12)

Satan – "Then Peter said, 'Ananias, how is it that **Satan** has so filled your heart that you have lied to the Holy Spirit and have kept for yourself some of the money you received for the land?" (Acts 5:3) (II Thessalonians 2:9) (Revelation 12:9)

Scoffers – "Look, you **scoffers**, wonder and perish, for I am going to do something in your days that you would never believe, even if someone told you." (Acts 13:41) "First of all, you must understand that in the last days **scoffers** will come, **scoffing** and following their own evil desires. They will say, 'Where is this 'coming' he promised? Ever since our fathers died, everything goes on as it has since the beginning of creation.' But they deliberately forget that long ago by God's word the heavens existed and the earth was formed out of water and by water. By these waters also the world of that time was deluged and destroyed. By the same word the present heavens and earth are reserved for fire, being kept for the Day of Judgment and destruction of ungodly men." (II Peter 3:3-7)

Sinfulness – "For when we were controlled by the **sinful** nature, the **sinful** passions aroused by the law were at work in our bodies, so that we bore fruit for death." (Romans 7:5) "The mind of **sinful** man is death, but the mind controlled by the Spirit is life, and peach; the **sinful** mind is hostile to God. It does not submit to God's law, nor can it do so. Those controlled by the **sinful** nature cannot please God." (Romans 8:6-7) "But avoid foolish controversies and genealogies and arguments and quarrels about the law, because these are unprofitable and useless. Warn a divisive person once, and then warn him a second time. After the, have nothing to do with him you may be sure that such a man is warped and **sinful**; he is self-condemned." (Titus 3:11)

Sorcerers – "'So I will come near to you for judgment. I will be quick to testify against **sorcerers**, adulterers and perjurers, against those who defraud laborers of their wages, who oppress the widows and the fatherless, and deprive aliens of justice, but do not fear me' says the Lord Almighty." (Malachi 3:5) "They traveled through the whole island until they came to Paphos. There they met a Jewish **sorcerer** and false prophet named Bar-Jesus who was an attendant of the proconsul, Sergius Paulus. The proconsul, an intelligent man, sent for Barnabas and Saul because he wanted to hear the word of God. But Elymas the **sorcerer** (for that is what his name means) opposed them and tried to turn the proconsul from the faith." (Acts 13:6-8)

Witchcraft – "I will destroy your witchcraft and you will no longer cast spells." (Micah 5:12) "Woe to the city of blood…all because of the wanton lust of a harlot, alluring, the mistress of sorceries, who enslaved nations by her prostitution and peoples by her **witchcraft**." (Nahum 3:1-4) "The acts of the sinful nature are obvious…idolatry and **witchcraft**…I warn you as I did before, that those who live like this will not inherit the kingdom of God." (Galatians 5:19-21)

Evil

For further study: Books of Psalm and Proverbs, Matthew chapter 5

Jesus not only warns us about the evil in the world, but he also gives us guidance as to dealing with the evil that comes upon us. He says, 'You have heard that it was said, 'Eye for eye, and tooth for tooth.' But I tell you, Do not resist an evil person. If someone strikes you on the right cheek, turn to him the other also, and if someone wants to sue you and take your tunic, let him have you cloak as well. If someone forces you to go one mile, go with him two miles. Give to the one who asks you, and do not turn away from the one who wants to borrow from you. You have heard that it was said, 'Love you neighbor and hate you enemy.' But I tell you: Love you enemies and pray for those who persecute you, that you may be sons of you Father in heaven. He causes His sun to rise on the evil and the good, and sends rain on the righteous and the unrighteous. If you love those who love you, what reward will you get? Are not even the tax collectors doing that? And if you greet only your brothers, what are you doing more than others? Do not even pagans do that? Be perfect, therefore, as you heavenly Father is perfect." (Matthew 5:38-48) Christ has set a goal which we cannot possibly surpass, that of being perfect. We know that God and Christ are perfect and without sin. Paul tells us his goal: "I want to know Christ and the power of His resurrection and the fellowship of sharing in His sufferings, becoming like Him in His death, and so, somehow, to attain to the resurrection from the dead." (Philippians 3:10-11) This would include the putting off of all evil in our lives.

Boasting – "In his arrogance the wicked man hunts down the weak, who are caught in the schemes he devises. He **boasts** of the craving of his heart;

he blesses the greedy and reviles the Lord." (Psalm 10:2-3) "This is what the Lord says: 'Let not the wise man **boast** of his wisdom or the strong man **boast** of his strength or the rich man **boast** of his riches, but let him who **boasts boast** about this: that he understands and knows me, that I am the Lord, who exercises kindness, justice and righteousness on earth, for in these I delight,' declares the Lord." (Jeremiah 9:23-24) "As it is you **boast** and brag. All such **boasting** is evil." (James 4:16) "These men are grumblers and faultfinders; they follow their own evil desires; they **boast** about themselves and flatter others for their own advantage." (Jude 1:16)

Contempt – "Let their lying lips be silenced, for with pride and **contempt** they speak arrogantly against the righteous." (Psalm 31:18) "Or do you show **contempt** for the riches of His kindness, tolerance and patience, not realizing that God's kindness leads you toward repentance?" (Romans 2:24)

Depravity – "...Since they did not think it worthwhile to retain the knowledge of God, He gave them over to a **depraved** mind, to do what ought not to be done. They have become filled with every kind of wickedness, evil, greed and **depravity**. They are full of envy, murder, strife, deceit and malice. They are gossips, slanderers, God-haters, insolent, arrogant and boastful; they invent ways of doing evil...." (Romans 1: 28-30) "Do everything without complaining or arguing, so that you may become blameless and pure, children of God without fault in a crooked and **depraved** generation in which you shine like stars in the universe...." (Philippians 2:14-15)

Evil deeds (Wicked deeds) – "Let not my heart be drawn to what is **evil**, to take part in **wicked deeds** with men who are **evil**doers; let me not eat of their delicacies." (Psalm 141:1) "The **evil deeds** of a wicked man ensnare him; the cords of his sin hold him fast." (Proverbs 5:22) "This is the verdict: Light has come into the world, but men loved darkness instead of light because their **deeds** were **evil**. Everyone who does **evil** hates the light, and will not come into the light for fear that his **deeds** will be exposed. (John 3:19-20)

Evil doers- "Will **evildoers** never learn—those who devour my people as men eat bread and who do not call on the Lord? There they are overwhelmed with dread, for God is present in the company of the righteous. You **evildoers** frustrate the plans of the poor, but the Lord is their refuge." (Psalm14:4-6) "Many will say to me on that day, 'Lord, did we not prophesy in your name, and in your name drive out demons and perform many miracles?' then I will tell them plainly, 'I never knew you. Away from me, you **evildoers!**' " (Matthew 7:22-23)

Evil one – "Simply let you 'Yes' be 'Yes' and your 'No' be 'No'; anything beyond this comes from the **evil one.**" (Matthew 13:19) "The weeds are the sons of the **evil one**, and the enemy who sows them is the devil. The harvest is the end of the age, and the harvesters are angels." (Matthew 13:38-39) "We know that we are the children of God, and that the whole world is under the control of the **evil one.**" (I John 5:19)

Evil spirits – "Then Jesus went around teaching from village to village. Calling the Twelve to Him, He sent them out two by two and gave them power over **evil spirits.**" (Mark 6:7) "With shrieks, **evil spirits** came out of many, and many paralytics and cripples were healed." (Acts 8:7) "Then I saw three **evil spirits** that looked like frogs; they came out of the mouth of the dragon, out of the mouth of the beast and out of the mouth of the false prophet." (Revelation 16:13)

Folly – "A prudent man keeps his knowledge to himself, but the heart of fools blurts out **folly.**" (Proverbs 12:23) "**Folly** delights a man who lacks judgment, but a man of understanding keeps a straight course." (Proverbs 15:21) "For the fool speaks **folly,** his mind is busy with evil: He practices ungodliness and spreads error concerning the Lord; the hungry he leaves empty and from the thirsty he withholds water." (Isaiah 32:6) "But they will not get very far because, as in the case of those men, their **folly** will be clear to everyone." (II Timothy 3:9)

Forces of evil – "For our struggle is not against flesh and blood, but against the rulers, against the authorities, against the powers of this dark world and against the spiritual **forces of evil** in the heavenly realm." (Ephesians 6:12)

Heart – "Men of perverse **heart** shall be far from me; I will have nothing to do with evil." (Psalm 101:4) "But the things that come out of the mouth come from the **heart**, and these make a man 'unclean.' For out of the **heart** come evil thoughts, murder, adultery, sexual immorality, theft, false testimony, slander. These are what make a man 'unclean'; but eating with unwashed hands does not make him 'unclean.' " (Matthew 15:18-19) "The good man brings forth good things out of the good stored up in his **heart**, and the evil man brings evil things out of the evil stored up in his **heart**. For out of the overflow of his **heart** his mouth speaks." (Luke 6:45)

Malice – "Do not drag me away with the wicked, with those who do evil, who speak cordially with their neighbors but harbor **malice** in their hearts." (Psalm 28:3) "For this is what the Sovereign Lord says: Because you have clapped your hands and stamped your feet, rejoicing with all the **malice** of your heart against the land of Israel, therefore I will stretch out my hand against you and give you as plunder to the nations. I will cut you off from the nations and exterminate you from the countries. I will destroy you, and you will know that I am the Lord." (Ezekiel 25:6-7) "Therefore let us keep the festival, not with the old yeast, the yeast of **malice** and wickedness, but with bread without yeast, the bread of sincerity and truth." (I Corinthians 5:8)

Revenge (Avenging) – "Therefore the Lord, the Lord Almighty, the Mighty One of Israel, declares: 'Ah, I will get relief from my foes and **avenge** myself on my enemies.' " (Isaiah 1:24) "Do not take **revenge**, my friends, but leave room for God's wrath, for it is written: 'It is mine to **avenge**; I will repay,' says the Lord." (Romans 12:19)

Repayment of evil – "Do not **repay** anyone **evil** for **evil**. Be careful to do what is right in the eyes of everybody." (Romans 12:17) "Do not repay **evil** with **evil** or insult with insult, but with blessing, because to this you were called so that you may inherit a blessing." (I Peter 3:9)

Speech – "To fear the Lord is to hate evil; I hate pride and arrogance, evil behavior and perverse **speech**." (Proverbs 8:13) "A scoundrel plots evil, and his **speech** is like a scorching fire." (Proverbs 16:27) "For, 'Whoever would love life and see good days must keep his tongue from evil and his lips from deceitful **speech**.' " (I Peter 3:10)

Stored-up evil – "The good man brings good things out of the good stored up in him, and the **evil** man brings **evil** things out of the **evil stored up** in him." (Matthew 12:35)

The world – "I will punish **the world** for its evil, the wicked for their sins. I will put an end to the arrogance of the haughty and will humble the pride of the ruthless." (Isaiah 13:11) "The world cannot hate you, but it hates me because I testify that what it does is evil." (John 7:7) "Through these He has given us His very great and precious promises, so that through them you may participate in the divine nature and escape the corruption in **the world** caused by evil desires." (II Peter 1:4)

Thoughts – "Let the wicked forsake his way and the evil man his **thoughts**. Let him turn to the Lord, and He will have mercy on him, and to our God, for He will freely pardon." (Isaiah 55:7) "Their feet rush into sin; they are swift to shed innocent blood. Their **thoughts** are evil **thoughts**; ruin and destruction mark their ways." (Isaiah 59:7) "Knowing their thoughts, Jesus said, 'Why do you entertain evil thoughts in your hearts.' " (Matthew 9:4) "Suppose a man comes into your meeting wearing a gold ring and fine clothes, and a poor man in shabby clothes also comes in. If you show special attention to the man wearing fine clothes and say, 'Here's a good seat for you,' but say to the poor man, 'You stand there' or 'Sit on the floor by my feet,' have you not discriminated among yourselves and become judges with evil **thoughts**?" (James 2:2-4)

Wickedness – "He will repay them for their sins and destroy them for their **wickedness**; the Lord out God will destroy them." (Psalm 94:23) "When **wickedness** comes, so does contempt, and with shame comes disgrace." (Proverbs 18:3) "When I say to a **wicked** man, 'You will surely die,' and you do not warn him or speak out to dissuade him from his evil ways in order to save his life, that **wicked** man will die for his sin, and I will hold you accountable for his blood. But if you do warn the **wicked** man and he does not turn from his **wickedness** or from his evil ways, he will die for his sin; but you will have saved yourself." (Ezekiel 3:18-19)

Hatred

For further study: Books of Matthew, I John, and Revelation

Hatred is the top rung on the ladder of the unbeliever. This is not to say that every unsaved person will have total hatred in their hearts, but those who have reached this point seem to be the most evil people in the world. They have no care in their hearts for either God or fellow man. This chapter will outline not only the characteristics of hatred, but also the punishments that are in store for all of those who do not believe that God gave His Son that all may have redemption through Him. This outline will also demonstrate that this hatred is between people, nations, governments, and finally between man and God. The Bible tells us, "He will punish those who do not know God and do not obey the gospel of our Lord Jesus. They will be punished with everlasting destruction and shut out from the presence of the Lord and from the majesty of His power...." (II Thessalonians 1:8-9)

Brothers – "Anyone who claims to be in the light but hates his **brother** is still in the darkness. Whoever loves his **brother** lives in the light, and there is nothing in him to make him stumble. But whoever hates his **brother** is in the darkness and walks around in the darkness; he does not know where he is going, because the darkness has blinded him." (I John 2:9-11) "This is the message you heard from the beginning: We should love one another. Do not be like Cain, who belonged to the evil one and murdered his **brother**. And why did he murder him? Because his own actions were evil and his **brother's** were righteous. Do not be surprised, my **brothers**, if the world hates you. We know that we have passed from death to life, because we love our **brothers**. Anyone who does not love remains in death. Anyone who hates his **brother** is a murderer, and you know that no murderer has eternal life in him." (I John 3:11-15) "If anyone says, 'I love God,' yet hates his **brother**, he is a liar. For anyone who does not love his **brother**, whom he has seen, cannot love God, whom he has not seen. And He has given us this command: Whoever loves God must also love his **brother**." (I John 4:20)

Condemnation – "Whoever believes in Him is not **condemned**, but whoever does not believe stands **condemned** already because he has not believed in the name of God's One and Only Son." (John 3:18) "The coming of the lawless one will be in accordance with the work of Satan displayed in all kinds of counterfeit miracles, signs and wonders, and in every sort of evil that deceives those who are perishing. They perish because they refused to love the truth and so be saved. For this reason God sends them a powerful delusion so that they will be believe the lie and so that all will be **condemned** who have not believed the truth but have delighted in wickedness." (II Thessalonians 2:9-12)

Day of Judgment – "But I tell you, it will be more bearable for Tyre and Sidon on the **Day of Judgment** than for you. And you, Capernaum, will you be lifted up to the skies? No, you will go down to the depths. If the miracles that were performed in you had been performed in Sodom, it would have remained to this day. But I tell you that it will be more bearable for Sodom on the **Day of Judgment** than for you." (Matthew 11:22-24) "But I tell you that men will have to give account on the **Day of Judgment** for every careless word they have spoken. For by you words you will be acquitted, and by your words you will be condemned." (Matthew 12:36-37) "But they deliberately forget that long ago by God's word the heavens existed and the earth was formed out of water and by water. By these same waters also the world of that time was deluged and destroyed. By the same word the present heavens and earth are reserved for fire, being kept for the **Day of Judgment** and destruction of ungodly men." (II Peter 3:5-7)

Deception – "For false Christs and false prophets will appear and perform great signs and miracles to **deceive** even the elect—if that were possible." (Matthew 24:24) "When the thousand years are over, Satan will be released from his prison and will go out to **deceive** the nations in the four corners of the earth—Gog and Magog—to gather them for battle. In number they are like the sand on the seashore. They marched across the breadth of the earth and surrounded the camp of God's people, the city He loves. But fire came down from heaven and devoured them. And the devil, who **deceived** them, was thrown into the lake of burning sulfur, where the beast and the false prophet had been thrown. They will be tormented day and night for ever and ever." (Revelation 20:7-10)

Enemies – "The days will come upon you when your **enemies** will build an embankment against you and encircle you and hem you in on every side. They will dash you to the ground, you and the children within your walls. They will not leave one stone on another, because you did not recognize the time of God's coming to you." (Luke 19:43) "Then the end will come, when He hands over the kingdom to God the Father after He has destroyed all dominion, authority and power. For He must reign until He has put all His **enemies** under His feet. The last **enemy** to be destroyed is death. For He 'has put everything under His feet.' Now when it says that 'everything' has been put under Him, it is clear that this does not include God Himself, who put everything under Christ." (I Corinthians 15:24-27) "For, as I have told you before and now say again even with tears, many live as **enemies** of the cross of Christ." (Philippians 3:18) "Once you were alienated from God and were **enemies** in your minds because of your evil behavior." (Colossians 1:21)

Eternal punishment (Everlasting destruction) – "Then they will go away to **eternal punishment**, but the righteous to eternal life." (Matthew 25:46) "He will **punish** those who do not know God and do not obey the gospel of our Lord Jesus. They will be **punished** with **everlasting destruction** and shut out from the presence of the Lord and from the majesty of His power on the day He comes to be glorified in His holy people and to be marveled at among all those who have believed. This includes you, because you believed our testimony to you." (II Thessalonians 1:8-10)

Evil doers – "The Son of Man will send out His angels, and they will weed out of His kingdom everything that causes sin and all who **do evil**. They will throw them into the fiery furnace, where there will be weeping and gnashing of teeth." (Matthew 13:41) "But He will reply, 'I don't know you or where you come from. Away from me, all you **evildoers**.' " (Luke 13:27) "Everyone who **does evil** hates the light, and will not come into the light for fear that his deeds will be exposed." (John 3:20)

God-haters – "They have become filled with every kind of wickedness, evil, greed and depravity. They are full of envy, murder, strife, deceit and malice. They are gossips, slanderers, **God-haters**, insolent, arrogant and boastful; they invent ways of doing evil; they disobey their parents; they are senseless, faithless, heartless, ruthless." (Romans 1:29-30)

Hate one another (Hate each other) – "Then you will he handed over to be persecuted and put to death, and you will be hated by all nations because of me. At that time many will turn away from the faith and will betray and **hate each other**...." (Matthew 24:9-10) "At that time, we too were foolish, disobedient, deceived and enslaved by all kinds of passions and pleasures. We lived in malice and envy, being **hated** and **hating one another**." (Titus 3:3)

Hatred – "The acts of the sinful nature are obvious: sexual immorality, impurity and debauchery; idolatry and witchcraft; **hatred**, discord, jealousy, fits of rage, selfish ambition, dissensions, factions and envy; drunkenness, orgies, and the like. I warn you, as I did before, that those who live like this will not inherit the kingdom of God." (Galatians 5:19-21) "You adulterous people, don't you know that friendship with the world is **hatred** toward God? Anyone who chooses to be a friend of the world becomes an enemy of God." (James 4:4)

Hatred of the Father and Son – "He who **hates** me hates my **Father** as well. If I had not done among them what no one else did, they would not be guilty of sin. But now they have seen these miracles, and yet they have **hated** both me and my **Father**. But this is to fulfill what is written in their Law: 'They **hated** me without reason.' " (John 15:23-25)

Hell – "Do not be afraid of those who kill the body but cannot kill the soul. Rather, be afraid of the One who can destroy both soul and body in **hell**." (Matthew 10:28) "You snakes! You brood of vipers! How will you escape being condemned to **hell**?" (Matthew 23:33) "For if God did not spare angels when they sinned, but sent them to **hell**, putting them into gloomy dungeons to be held for judgment; if He did not spare the ancient world when He brought the flood on its ungodly people, but protected Noah, a preacher of righteousness, and seven others; if He condemned the cities of Sodom and Gomorrah by burning them to ashes, and made them an example of what is going to happen to the ungodly; and if he rescued Lot, a righteous man, who was distressed by the filthy lives of lawless men (for that righteous man, living among them day after day, was tormented in his righteous soul by the lawless deeds he saw and heard)—if this is so, then the Lord knows how to rescue godly men from trials and gold the unrighteous for the day of judgment, while continuing their punishment. This is especially true of those who follow the corrupt desire of the sinful nature and despise authority...." (II Peter 2:4-10)

Mankind (Men) – "All **men** will hate you because of me, but he who stands firm to the end will be saved." (Matthew 10:22) "Blessed are you when **men** hate you, when they exclude you and insult you and reject you name as evil, because of the Son of Man. Rejoice in that day and leap for joy, because great is you reward in heaven. For that is how their fathers treated the prophets." (Luke 6:22) "All **men** will hate you because of me. But not a hair of you head will perish by standing firm you will gain life." (Luke 21:17)

Murderers – "You have heard that it was said to the people long ago, 'Do not **murder**, and anyone who **murders** will be subject to judgment.' But I tell you that anyone who is angry with his brother will be subject to judgment. Again, anyone who says to his brother, 'Raca,' is answerable to the Sanhedrin. But anyone who says, 'You fool!' will be in danger of the fire of hell." (Matthew 5:21) "You belong to your father, the devil, and you want to carry out your father's desire. He was a **murderer** from the beginning, not holding to the truth, for there is no truth in him. When he lies, he speaks his native language, for he is a liar and the father of lies." (John 8:44)

Nations (Kingdoms) – "**Nation** will rise against **nation**, and **kingdom** against **kingdom**. There will be famines and earthquakes in various places. All these are the beginning of birth pains. Then you will be handed over to be persecuted and put to death, and you will be hated by all **nations** because of me. At that time many will turn away from the faith and will betray and hate each other, and many false prophets will appear and deceive many people." (Matthew 24:7-9)

Second death – "...I am the Alpha and the Omega, the Beginning and the End. To him who is thirsty I will give to drink without cost from the spring of the water of life. He who overcomes will inherit all this, and I will be his God and he will be my son. But the cowardly, the unbelieving, the vile, the murderers, the sexually immoral, those who practice magic arts, the idolaters and all liars—their place will be in the fiery lake of burning sulfur. This is the **second death**." (Revelation 21:6-8)

The world – "If **the world** hates you, keep in mind that it hated me first. If you belonged to **the world**, it would love you as its own. As it is, you do not belong to **the world**, but I have chosen you out of **the world**. That is why **the world** hated you." (John 15:18-19) "I have given them your word and **the world** has hated them, for they are not of **the world** any more that I am of **the world**. My prayer is not that you take them out of **the world** but that you protect them from the evil one. They are not of **the world**, even as I am not of it." (John 17:14-16) "Do not be surprised, my brothers, if **the world** hates you. We know that we have passed from death to life, because we love our brothers. Anyone who does not love remains in death. Anyone who hates his brother is a murderer, and you know that no murderer has eternal life in Him." (I John 3:13)

Torment – "A third angel followed them and said in a loud voice: ' If anyone worships the beast and his image and receives his mark on the forehead or on the hand, he, too, will drink of the wine of God's fury, which has been poured full strength into the cup of His wrath. He will be **tormented** with burning sulfur in the presence of the holy angels and of the Lamb. And the smoke of their **torment** rises forever and ever. There is no rest day or night for those who worship the beast and him image, or for anyone who receives the mark of his name.' " (Revelation 14:9-11)

Two masters – "No one can serve **two masters**. Either he will hate the one and love the other, or he will be devoted to the one and despise the other. You cannot serve both God and Money." (Matthew 6:24) "No servant can serve **two masters**. Either he will hate the one and love the other, or he will be devoted to the one and despise the other. You cannot serve both God and Money." (Luke 16:13)

APPENDIX I

Attributes Which Strengthen Faith

ability
abounding
abstinence
abundance
acceptance
access
accountability
acknowledgement
admiration
adoption
adoration
advancement
advice
agreement
alertness
anointing
approval
armor of God
asking
assurance
atonement
balm
baptism
beauty
belief
belonging
blamelessness
blessings
boldness

brotherly kindness
brotherly love
calmness
care
character
charity
cheerfulness
child of God
chosen
clarity
cleansing
comfort
compassion
competence
completeness
comprehension
confession
confidence
conscience
consecration
contentment
conviction
dedication
delight
deliverance
devotion
diligence
discernment
discipleship

divine nature
edification
encouragement
endurance
enlightenment
exaltation
faith
faithfulness
fasting
favor
fearlessness
fellowship
forbearance
forgiveness
friendship
fruit
fullness
generosity
gentleness
gifts
giving
gladness
godliness
goodness
graciousness
happiness
helper
holiness
honor

hope
hospitality
humbleness
humility
insight
inspiration
integrity
joy
justice
kindness
knowledge
laughter
lawfulness
listener
love
loyalty
maturity
meditation
meekness
mercy
minister
modesty
obedience
offerings
overflowing
patience
peacefulness
peacemaker
perseverance
power
praise
prayerfulness
protector
provider
prudence
purity
purposefulness
quietness
readiness

reconciliation
regard
rejoicing
repentant
respectfulness
reverence
righteousness
sacrifice
sanctification
security
seeker
self-controlled
serving
sharing
sincerity
singing
spiritual maturity
studious
submissiveness
talented
teacher
tenderness
thankfulness
tolerance
transformed
triumphant
trustworthy
truthful
understanding
unity
victorious
virtuous
wholesome
wisdom
workman
worship
worthiness
zeal

Appendix II

Attributes Which Weaken Faith

abominations
abuse
accusations
addictions
adultery
adversity
afflictions
alienation
anger
anguish
anxiety
arguments
arrogance
babbling
backbiting
backsliding
bitterness
blaming
blasphemy
busybodies
carelessness
carnality
cheating
complacency
complaining
conceit
condemnation
conspiracy
controversies
corruption

covetousness
craftiness
cravings
criticism
cursing
darkness
debauchery
deceit
deceivers
defiling
defrauding
delusions
demons
depravity
desolation
desperation
despising
destroying
destruction
deviousness
disagreements
discord
discouragement
diseases
disfiguring
disgrace
dishonesty
dishonor
disillusionment
disobedience

disorder
disowning
disparity
displeasure
disputes
disrepute
dissensions
distortions
distress
divinations
divisions
divorce
doubt
drunkenness
enticements
envy
evil
evildoer
exasperation
excuses
exploiting
failure
faithlessness
falsehoods
faultfinding
fear
fighting
filthiness
flattery
folly

foolishness	lawlessness	sexual sin
fools	laziness	shame
fornication	liars	slander
friction	lust	sorcery
fruitlessness	malice	stealing
fury	meddlers	strife
futility	misdeeds	swindling
gloating	misleading	tattoos
gluttony	misusing	temptations
gnashing of teeth	mocking	theft
God-haters	murder	torment
godlessness	name-calling	traitors
gossips	obscenity	transgressions
greed	oppression	treachery
grievances	orgies	trespasses
grumbling	partiality	trickery
guilt	perjury	unbelief
hatred	persecution	unworthiness
haughtiness	perversion	unfruitfulness
heathenism	pride	ungodliness
hindering	profaning	ungraciousness
hoarding	prostitution	unholiness
homosexuality	quarreling	unproductivity
hopelessness	rage	unrighteousness
hostility	rebellion	unruliness
humiliation	rejection	unspirituality
hypocrisy	resentment	uselessness
idleness	retaliation	usury
idolatry	revenge	violence
ignorance	robbery	wastefulness
immorality	Satanism	wickedness
impurity	schemes	witchcraft
indecency	scoffers	worldliness
indifference	scorn	worry
iniquity	scorn	wrath
injustice	scoundrels	wrong-doing
insolence	self-indulgence	uncleanness
insults	selfishness	unfaithfulness
irreligiousness	self-seeking	unforgiveness
jealousy	sensuality	

GLOSSARY

Abandoning God/faith – turning away from the teachings of God; choosing to live one's own lifestyle

Abstinence – to refrain from or refuse to partake

Acceptance – to agree to something like a belief; to acknowledge as truth

Access – availability; able to approach; open to something

Affection – strong favorable feelings; close emotionally

Affliction – mental or physical difficulty

Angel of light (Satan) – Satan's claim to being like God or angel; a pretense that Satan is good

Anger – hostility or strong displeasure

Anguish – mental suffering

Anxiety – being uncomfortable or anxious about something

Approval – acceptance; looking upon something favorably

Arrogance – pride; superiority; insolence

Asking – making a request; petitioning

Assurance – a feeling of security or safety; confidence in something

Atonement – payment; suffering some else's penalty for wrong doing

Baptism – emersion; dedication or acknowledgement of belief

Baptism of the Holy Spirit – the in-dwelling of the Holy Spirit after a person is saved

Beauty of Holiness – the wonderful aspects of being more like God; having a different view of life

Beelzebub – one of Satan's demons, perhaps derived from Ba'al and Ba'al worship

Behavior – the manner in which one conducts oneself; demeanor

Belief – acceptance as truth; sincere faith

Benevolence – kindness toward other people; doing something for someone in need

Blameless – having no guilt; innocent

Blasphemy – swearing; irreverence; speaking out against God

Blindness – physical or mental condition or not seeing or understanding

Boasting – bragging; self-praise; crediting oneself with an accomplishment

Bodily sin – any sin within the body of a person; sinful or non-spiritual uses of the human body

Book of Life – a recording of the names of saved people

Born Again – not only born physically, but also spiritually

Brotherly love – compassion for those in need

Brothers – fellow believers; fellow Christians

Burdens – heavy loads; concerns; mental anguish

Care – concern; having favorable feelings

Carousing – drinking of alcoholic beverages; partying

Certainty – being absolutely sure about something

Charity – love; giving of oneself to those in need

Children of God – those belonging to God

Christ's blood – the sacrificial blood which was shed for the sins of all mankind

Christian – one who identifies with Christ as Savior

Christian friends – others who identify with Christ

Cleanness (Cleanliness) – without sin, blot, or blemish

Cleansing – the process of making one clean

Comfort – being at peace with both God and oneself

Commands (Commandments) – orders from God

Compassion – concern for those in need; love

Competence – physical or mental capability

Complaining – voicing negative feelings

Concern – personal interest; care; favorable feeling

Condemnation – judgment against someone; spiritual death

Confidence – self assurance; belief in someone else

Conforming – agreeing with; following; pattern oneself after another

Confusion – lack of clarity; mentally unclear

Conquerors – those who come out victorious

Conscience – one's inner feelings or recognition

Consecration – dedication; making holy or sacred

Consolation – providing comfort to one in grief

Contempt – despising or having bad feelings about

Contentment – inner satisfaction; moral comfort

Conversation – communication with others or God

Conviction – absolute belief; a surety

Corruption – immoral; without spiritual values

Counsel – giving advice; recommendations

Courage – intestinal fortitude; bravery

Cravings – strong wishes or desires; lusting

Created things – things made by God during Creation; things made by the hands of men

Criticism – fault finding; accusing; blaming

Cunning – cleverness; deceitfulness

Cursing – blaspheming; denouncing; degrading

Darkness – physical or spiritual ignorance

Day of Judgment – the end of this age when the saved and separated from the unsaved

Death – physical or spiritual termination

Debauchery – sexual seduction

Debt – something owed to a person or to God

Deception – concealment of the truth; trickery

Delusion – making something seem real

Demon – an agent of Satan; immoral being

Denial – refusal to believe; speaking disbelief

Depravity – degrading behavior; immorality

Detestable things – things unclean in God's view

Devil – Satan; enemy of both God and mankind

Devotion – deep, positive commitment to God

Diligence – great care; careful attention

Disbelief – refusing to accept as truth or fact

Discernment – ability to understand

Discretion – ability to use one's own judgment

Dishonest gain – illegal and immoral asset

Disobedience – refusal to practice or comply

Dissension – argument; disagreement; conflict

Divine Nature – a nature like God; spiritual

Divine Power – power possessed or given by God

Doctrine – teachings; beliefs; principles

Doubt – being unsure; having reservations

Drunkenness – intoxication; not sober

Earthly nature – human; not from God

Edification – building up; strengthening; spiritual awareness

Encouragement – motivation; inspiration

Endurance – ability to continue through hardship

Enemies – those opposed to God and His ways

Enlightenment – insight; acquired knowledge

Envy – jealousy; covetous

Eternal Life – life without end; existing forever

Eternal punishment – unending penalty

Evil deeds – things done against God's will

Evil desires – human cravings; not seeking God

Evil doers – those who act against God's will

Evil one – Satan; the devil

Evil spirits – spirits under Satan's control

Example – person or thing to be followed

Exercise – to put into use; to carry out

Faithfulness – complete obedience to God

False apostle – person pretending to follow God

False brother – those who do not truly believe

False Christ – untruthful pretender

False doctrine – teaching not according to God

False images – counterfeits; untrue symbols

False prophets – those who spread false doctrine

False teachers – those who teach lies as truth

False testimony – things espoused to be true but are actually have no substance

False witness – one who lies about actual events

Falsehood – a lie; purposeful deceit

Fear – dread; terror; alarm

Fellowship – union of believers; pleasing association

Flattery – undue compliments

Folly – foolish behavior

Foolishness – things done without due thought

Force of evil – the power of Satan and his followers

Forgiveness – pardon without payment or penalty

Fulfillment – completion of prophecy; fruition

Fullness – completion; with nothing lacking

Gentleness – tenderness; kindness; softness

Gift of God – God's fulfilled promises to mankind

Gifts – those presents for which we make no payment

Giving – loving; caring; a gift

Glory – greatness; praise; joy

Goats – those who are unsaved

God's patience – God's willingness to wait

God's will – God's desire for us

God-haters – those who turn completely from God

Godless chatter – many words with little meaning

Godliness – holiness; without blemish; sacredness

Grace – forgiveness; compassion; favor

Gratification – satisfying one's own desires

Graven image – carved or molten likeness

Great Faith – faith beyond the ordinary; extreme faith

Great Worth – of eternal value

Greatest Love – sacrificial love; blood sacrifice

Greed – wanting more than is needed

Hardened heart – one that completely turns from God; lacking in compassion or feeling

Hardship – difficulty; something not easily overcome

Hatred – extreme evil feeling; extreme dislike

Healing – something that cures; something that makes whole again

Hearing – physical or spiritual ability to understand

Heart – the seat of emotions; the spiritual center of a person

Hell – place of punishment and torment

Helping – giving aid; supporting

Holiness – spirituality; godliness

Holy Spirit (Holy Ghost) – the indwelling of God's Spirit

Honesty – uprightness; complete candidness

Hope – aspiration; to look forward to

Hospitality – graciousness; receiving of guests

Hostility – evil feelings; enmity; hatred

Humility – humbleness; modesty

Hunger – desire for God; desire for knowledge

Idleness – inactivity; without ambition; not working

Idol worship – anything regarded higher than God

Idolatry – the worship of man-made images

Ignorance – lack of knowledge of the truth

Ignoring – choosing not to recognize existence

Immorality – things against the will of God

Impurity – things unclean in the sight of God

Indecent acts – things unacceptable to God

Indulgence – participation; taking pleasure in

Infidel – a non-Christian; an unbeliever

Insight – above normal understanding

Instruction – teaching; imparting knowledge

Insulting the spirit – speaking against the Holy Spirit

Insults – intentional verbal abuse, often against Christians

Integrity – spiritual strength; being honest

Interests – things to increase one's well being

Irreligious – things done or spoken against God

Jealousy – envy; resentment

Jesus' Love – the greatest possible affection

Judging – deciding; ruling; condemning

Justification – defense of one's actions; supporting

Kindness – affectionate and helping attitude

Kingdom – the area or domain over which one rules

Lacking self-control – inability to make good decisions for oneself

Lawbreakers – transgressors; sinners

Learning – obtaining knowledge or awareness

Liars – one who tells lies; a false witness

Liberation – freedom; to be set free of sin

Lies – anything which alters the truth

Life – both physical and spiritual being; existence

Light – intellectual knowledge; insight

Listen – make an effort to hear and comprehend

Longsuffering – the ability to endure hardship without complaining

Love – the greatest of all affections towards another

Love of money – placing the value of money above all else

Lovers of themselves – total self-interest; selfishness

Lusts of the flesh – satisfying human desires over the will of God

Magic arts – trickery; sorcery; witchcraft; deception

Malice – evil feelings towards God or mankind

Mankind – humanity; fellow human beings

Maturity – full physical or spiritual growth

Meditate – ponder; think over; consider

Mock – ridicule; make fun of; imitate

Mystery – things that God has hidden; things that God has chosen to reveal only to Christians

Neglect – ignoring an important responsibility; disregard;

Neighbor – any person in need; fellow being

Never Failing – something that always achieves positive results

New Creature (New Life) – God's salvation through Jesus Christ

Not hearing – physically or spiritually not listening or not paying attention

Obedience – full compliance; willingly carrying out God's will

Obstinacy – stubbornness; unyielding; not surrendering

Orgy – cult worship; wrongful participation in drunkenness or sexual activity

Pagans – a person with no religious beliefs

Passion – strong emotion or desire

Peace – inner calmness; knowing that God is near

Pentecost – a celebration of the Christian church occurring on the seventh Sabbath Day after Easter

Perfection – without fault or flaw; excellence in quality

Persecution – purposeful malice towards believers

Persecution of Saints – malice towards God's chosen

Perseverance – continuing one's course despite hardship

Perversion – wrongful or corrupt use of something

Poisoned minds – destruction of all mental capacity

Poisonous lips (tongue) – destructive speech

Prayer – oral or silent communication with God; meditation

Profitability – anything that has appositive outcome

Promise – covenant; guarantee

Purification – complete spiritual cleansing

Quarrel – fuss; disagreement; often a heated debate

Rage – uncontrolled outbursts; violent anger

Redemption – rescue from all sins; complete forgiveness

Refuse – not to accept; deny; turn down an offer

Reject – turn down an offer; refuse to accept

Rejoicing – spiritual celebration

Remembering (Remembrance) – commemoration; celebration; acknowledgment

Renewing – refreshing; making like new again

Repayment of evil – revenge; avenging someone who has wronged you; punishment

Repentance – asking and receiving God's forgiveness for sins

Reprobate mind (Depraved mind) – a mind completely controlled by the sinful nature

Respect – politeness; agreement; comply with

Revelation – knowledge gained directly through God's intervention

Revenge – taking action against one who has wronged another; vindictiveness; retaliation

Reverence – highest respect toward God; sacredness

Reward – promise of something yet to come; honor

Riches – God's blessings to mankind; silver, gold, or other substances considered valuable by mankind

Righteousness – without purposeful sin; likeness to God

Sabbath-rest – not participating in daily activities on the Sabbath; dedication to the Lord on the Sabbath

Sacredness – held in highest esteem; holiness

Sacrifice – giving up (as in one's life); willing obedience to God's will

Salvation – rescue from danger or punishment

Sanctification – the act of making holy or sacred

Satan – the devil; personification of evil

Scoffer – one who makes fun of or rebukes another

Scripture – any portion of the written Word of God

Second death – eternal punishment; spiritual death

Security – safety; something of great value

Self-control – ability to keep intact one's behaviors and emotions

Self-indulgence – desire to satisfy human craving

Selfish ambition – desire to satisfy personal goals rather than godly goals

Sensuality – suggestive or sexual behavior

Separation – isolation; keeping apart; division

Service – a duty; act of putting into use

Sexual immorality – wrongful sexual behavior

Share – willing to give up to satisfy another's need

Shedding of Blood – Christ's willingness to die for the sins of all mankind

Sheep – those willing to follow God's will; followers

Sin – wrongful behavior; breaking God's covenant

Sinful desires (Sinful nature) –

Sinful nature – desire to fulfill human desires

Slander – speech intended to harm another

Slaves to sin – under the control of Satan rather than God

Sorcery – practice of deception through satanic power

Sorrow – sadness; grief; pain caused by a loss

Spirit – a divine being; inner self; the soul

Spirit of Truth - God's guidance and control

Spiritual food – nourishment from God; strength

Spirituality – under the control of God, not mankind

Standing firm – not wavering; upright behavior

Stealing – taking wrongful possession; theft

Stillness – quiet observance; solitude; meditation

Stored-up evil – unforgiveness in one's heart

Strength – power from God; source of endurance

Study – application for learning; concentration; careful examination

Submission – bowing to God's will

Suffering – willing endurance of hardships

Swindler – one who gains through deception

Teacher – educator; one who instructs in righteousness

Teaching – imparting knowledge to the unlearned

Temper – a tendency to become angry

Temptation – something that attracts with a promise of pleasure

Tenderness – love; caring; consideration

Testify – to state as truth; revelation of reality

Thankfulness – outward appreciation; gratefulness

The Way – group of Christian believers; probably a reference to Jesus as the Way, Truth, and Life

The world – a reference to unsaved mankind

Thirst – desire or truth; eagerness to be filled

Tithe – giving of one-tenth of everything to God

Tongue – the instrument of speaking either good or evil

Torment – punishment; torture; suffering

Transformation – inner and outer change through salvation

Transgression – disobedience to God's commands

Trespasses – sins; transgressions; breaking promises

Trial – examination of obedience; burden

Tribulation – eternal punishment; distress; affliction

Trouble – problem; danger; difficulty

Trust – absolute dependence; complete belief

Truth – undisputable fact; God Himself

Unbelief – refusal to accept as truth; disbelief

Understand – comprehend; know as fact or truth

Unforgiving – condition of continued guilt

Unity – oneness; spiritual togetherness

Unrepentant – refusal to confess; not forgiven

Unspiritual – complete lack of godly attributes

Victory – spiritual success; overcoming of evil

Virtue – the goodness provided by God

Waiting upon God – abiding one's time for God's direction; following godly virtues

Walking in darkness – living without God; lacking spiritual direction

Wandering from faith – being drawn away from God

Weakness – submission to ungodly behavior

Weariness – physical weakness; lack of strength

Wickedness – evil; controlled by Satan; sinfulness

Wild living – uncontrolled waste of life or money

Wisdom – the application of godly knowledge

Witchcraft – sorcery; deception; use of evil spirits

Workman (Worker) – one who is under God's control

Worldly Love – passion for human desires rather than God's will

Worry – unnecessary concern; anxiety

Worship – adoration and praise of God

Zeal – enthusiasm; passionate desire

CPSIA information can be obtained at www.ICGtesting.com
Printed in the USA
238329LV00002B/3/P